Published by: Capucia, LLC
211 Pauline Drive #513
York, PA 17402

Paperback ISBN: 978-0-9968271-6-4
eBook ISBN: 978-0-9968271-7-1
Library of Congress Control Number: 2021901837

Cover Illustrator: Natalia Moroz
Layout: Ranilo Cabo
Editor: Appio Hunter
Proofreader: MJ Schwader
Book Midwife: Carrie Jareed

Printed in the United States of America

My Calling
My Quest

Truth

C.W. Isaac

For

Beautiful Humanity,

and those who collaborate on their behalf

for their attainment of peace.

Contents

Truth Disclosure

My Calling, My Quest's number one goal is providing Humanity access to their Truths. This is its primary purpose since Truth was not destined for only a select few. With presenting Truth, though, there is a responsibility to disclose its effects. Therefore, to meet that standard, I inform you that the Truths within will not only shift your perspective, they will also advance your Awakening. With that conveyed, please thoughtfully consider your readiness to receive Truth's powerful, transformative abilities.

Truth…

It is that which reveals the origin of whom we are

and how all existing came into existence.

Dear Reader,

Before we begin, there are a couple of items to mention.

The first is, I have moved the traditional Introduction to the back of this book. I made this choice because, for some readers, an Introduction disrupts their entire experience. The feedback was that "it ruins an enjoyable read." For others, though, when a book provides an opportunity for profound transformation, they feel guidance in how to proceed is essential to their experience.

Therefore, to create an optimal outcome for everyone, you can proceed in one of two ways: continue reading to discern this book's intentions and goals for yourself, or turn to the Addendum, which is where you will find the Introduction. The Addendum's exact location appears in the Table of Contents. In the Table of Contents, you will also find where the Glossary is located; this I provide to assist with your assimilation of the topics presented.

Please note, though you can forgo the Introduction, you may want to consider otherwise as I address questions that can enhance your reading experience. For instance, what are you supposed to do with your Truths, and how can you put them to use? Either way, sit back, relax, and enjoy your read, beginning with the Author's Note, as it provides the basis for My Calling, My Quest's entire purpose.

The additional item to mention is that My Calling, My Quest (Truth) is but one part of a greater work and purpose. That is, what you have in hand is not the entire manuscript. Instead, it only contains a portion of the Truth, Clarity, and Hope I am here to deliver. This indicates Humanity's Truths are releasing prior to the remainder. The reason for this is because it was determined Humanity needed their Truths immediately. Their Awakening experience is quickly unfolding, and the current conflicts on Earth are begging for factual transparency.

When will My Calling, My Quest (Clarity and Hope) publish? Soon, within a year's time from the date of this initial publication. You can visit www.MyCallingMyQuest.com for release updates and additional resources brought to you on behalf of this book's vision and mission. You can also visit this site to download a free PDF containing all illustrations and handouts found within for ease of readability.

In closing, I cannot begin to express how moved I am this day has come. My heart and soul goals are finally transpiring with these Truths making their way to you. The great news is, if I am accomplishing what I am on Earth to do, you can do the same. Follow my lead, open your heart, and consider embracing this way to peace.

That said, enjoy reading the insights offered within, and the incredible Truths of whom Humanity is.

With appreciation,

C.W. Isaac

Author's Note

In early 2014, Humanity embarked on a quest unlike any they had taken before. The venture rose from their Third Intention: to collectively awaken, for the achievement of peace on Earth.

Additionally, with their intention in place, Humanity determined they would need a plan of action to navigate their Awakening. Specifically, a means and way for them to collectively emerge from their unawakened state of consciousness.

With both decisions made, they then decided what the action plan for their Awakening needed: 1) Truth. Full disclosure regarding their historic account, from the place where nothing exists, to where every person resides on Earth today. 2) Clarity. The facts revealing how they descended in consciousness, highlighting their accountability for the conditions currently existing on Earth. 3) Hope. Detailed instruction on how to resolve their ongoing peace predicament.

Fast forward to 2020. Despite Humanity's insatiable desire to live harmoniously, they have yet to implement a comprehensive plan to reach that goal. In fact, this is Humanity's number one unsolved problem, which allows fear to continue ruling on Earth. Additionally, it allows deplorable conditions to thrive and survive. Are there solutions? Yes, there are. This includes the solution you will encounter within, aptly named—the *Awakening Plan for Peace*.

Deep within, we know peace is what our hearts desire most for all life existing on Earth. This desire is why *My Calling, My Quest* even exists. It is a book written to gift Humanity a way to awaken by way of their Truths. It is also a book with a unique presentation and purpose, having the ability to unite all people on Earth. An unlikely outcome? Absolutely not, since Humanity is already in the midst of an Awakening and effectively progressing as intended.

The question for you is, will you lead or will you follow? I believe if you are reading this, then you have stepped in to help lead the way. First, with your own transformation—*as it is key to achieving peace on Earth*—followed by you helping others navigate their conscious ascension. Either way, either path, I am honored you have joined me here today, and I look forward to all points of connection we share amid Humanity's pursuit for peace.

The following may seem fictitious, yet know it is real and true:

Your remarkable history, how you came to exist,
and an explanation as to why the world you live in is as it is.
Solutions are at hand for the ailing of all, having the ability to
advance peace on Earth.

With that disclosed and without further delay...
I welcome you to the fantastic, not so fictional, Truths and
possibilities of me, you, and Humanity too.

Chapter 1

Planet Fear

Long ago, from where I once served, I learned of a place far away. It was a Universe existing beyond our own, and its inhabitants were named Humanity. I observed them frequently, was fascinated with their uniqueness, and admired their exceptional experience: vibrant colors, artistic expressions, and remarkable exotic beings. The wonders and beauty of their world were the finest existing throughout all of creation.

Then the day came when chaos erupted, for reasons unfamiliar to me. Beyond perplexed, I frequently wondered what in their world had caused the shift? Darkness prevailed, *the Light* diminished, and the only evidence of their existence was their constant pleas for help. Concerned with their wellbeing, I searched high and low, yet I never solved their ongoing mystery. The reason is that where I am from, the source of their problem does not exist.

Many years later, where years are unknown, I agreed to assist Humanity. Upon my arrival at the place they call home, I discovered the cause of their troubles. Its name is fear, it is their greatest enemy, and it relentlessly plagues one and all: fear itself, one's personal fears, and the collective fears of Humanity.

Everyone on Earth is infected with fear, and all life suffers from it. Planetary destruction, resource depletion, and the extinction of incredible species. Warring, violence, human trafficking, poverty, disease, and starvation.

Though fear is the primary culprit, Humanity is culpable too. That's because they created fear, and then they fell unconscious. After that, things took a turn for the worse because they comingled their beliefs with their judgments.

Beliefs teeming with prejudice, provoking hate, and fueling racism. Beliefs that endlessly discriminate, no matter one's given circumstance: privileged or not; male, female, or non-gender; white, black, or cataloging humans according to color.

Then there are religious beliefs that cause additional harm. The beliefs humans continually use to shame and condemn one another. The non-believers, those who are uncertain, and even the believers themselves, continually debating who does it right, who does it wrong, who is most favored, and who will pay the price.

The situation on Earth is quite the quandary, messy too, and even though Humanity contributed—fear is at the root of their issue. Fear grew, thrived, became big and strong, and no one escapes its destruction. This, of course, is inclusive of me since Earth is where I currently serve.

Which of the fears has consumed me most? Humanity's, mine, or fear itself? Honestly, I do not know, because in the depths of its grip it was impossible to tell. What I do know is, when my mission commenced on Planet Earth… fear as a Foe took aim at me.

Fear as an adversary? Yes, it was my number one nemesis! In fact, only weeks prior to this writing, I was almost another casualty. Over time, fear has pressed me to quit my quest repeatedly; yet it was our most recent encounter that almost had me conceding entirely. It nearly had me abandoning all most meaningful to me, even though a *Mission Complete* was within reach.

Yes, fear came to fight the fight of all fights and nearly won by targeting my deepest weaknesses. The vulnerabilities common to us all that try to convince us we are capable of nothing at all. It silently approaches, then it loudly declares, "You're not good enough, you're incapable, and you are utterly unworthy. I know it, you know it, and everyone knows it's true."

If that fails to stop our forward progression, it parades our past trials, tribulations, and misgivings before us. We work tirelessly to overcome fear's abuse, and when we think we have succeeded—it strikes again! It keeps us awake, has us pacing the floor, and it chips away at us until it discovers how to gain access once more. It promised to destroy me if I did not step away, then it vowed what I was here to deliver would never see the light of day.

Why does fear behave this way? It is because it wants to maintain its rule, and it will use everything within its arsenal to do so. Fear has even toppled love's abilities and destroyed its entire purpose. This, sadly for all, is when love's reign on Earth ended.

Why has fear targeted me? It is because my job here is to use every resource I have at hand to end its rule. Fortunately, what I have in hand is what fear fears most: *Truth*. Additionally, a means and way for Humanity to awaken so fear can never govern again.

Impossible? Not in the least. Fear may have had the power to oust love and terminate peace, yet it has nothing within its reach to conquer Truth. This signifies, one day, love can rule again. However, the restoration of peace must come first—as without it love has no basis. Fortunately, peace is realistic and achievable. All Humanity must do is prioritize peace and utilize an agreed-upon course in how to awaken.

You may question the validity of what I share, yet I assure you, reaching peace on Earth is possible. I know this is Truth because it's my mission… it's my incredible calling and quest.

Chapter 2

Mission, Calling, and Quest

My calling and quest commenced in January 2014... the year I have deemed as the beginning of all beginnings since the beginning of Humanity's *modern-day* age. It was also the year when Humanity decided the time was now for them to awaken.

Who made that decision? Who had that right? The Mortal Majority, also known as the souls of humankind. Once they reached a decision, it catapulted the quests of many into the stratosphere of all existing. In fact, Humanity's decisive course is exactly when my highest mission began.

What is my mission? Entirely, it is to help Humanity ascend in consciousness within the realm they presently live. Currently, it is to create a viable way for them to awaken for the restoration of peace. I am to accomplish this all by tracking, mapping, organizing, and presenting Humanity's highest Truths.

Seriously? Yes! It is the only reason I exist.

What motivated me to take on this enormous task? The answer is quite simple: I was asked. First by the Mortal Majority (each of your souls) and then by whom afforded Humanity their exceptional experience. Their requests were issued eons ago when I lived far outside of Humanity's realm. That story is currently irrelevant, and the telling of it will have to wait—since the only thing of importance now is delivering the *Awakening Plan for Peace.*

Did I create this way to peace instantly, in 2014? Absolutely not, since it took my earthly mind months to recover from a massive transformation. That's because my consciousness expanded beyond recognition through a reconfiguration and rewiring process. Basically, when my calling catapulted into the stratosphere, my entire existence blew into bits and pieces. This was necessary and purposeful, so I could travel to dimensions I had not explored before.

Fantastic, right? In some ways, yes, in others no, since the event was the most overwhelming—*I think I might die*—experience I have ever encountered. In full disclosure, I was unsure I would survive any of it. Were those my first moments of living in high degrees of consciousness on Earth? No, since I came in awake so I can serve as I do—I call it being *unveiled.* That means *the veil* Humanity placed between themselves and higher consciousness has no blinding effects on me.

After recovering from the effects of conscious expansion, the great news is I was able to begin easing myself into the intention of my mission. During this time, while learning how to navigate my new reality, I was awkward at best. Awkward because while searching for a collaborative partner, I had to figure out how to explain the details of my calling. Initially, I naively disclosed far too much information. This, unfortunately, had many people shutting doors to collaboration, which is a requirement for the *Awakening Plan* to land.

Though there were many bumps along the way, fortunately, by summertime, a joy-filled, light-shining-bright collaborator agreed to assist. And because she did, *Operation Peace on Earth* launched. I took to the ethers mapping all Truths needed to fulfill my mission's intention. Meanwhile, she documented the facts I tracked regarding how all beings came into existence. Thank you, Miss Gwen Irwin, for serving with me, as without you, I am uncertain I would have found my way.

In spring the following year, with my initial findings documented, I formulated the principles that would serve as the foundation for the *Awakening Plan*. When complete, I realized the great things they were capable of. Specifically, their ability to facilitate peace. The principles, which evolved into a *Daily Practice for Peace*, are:

Start Being the Change, Today
Choose Your Stories Wisely
Love More than You Fear
Create Consciously and Responsibly
Seek the Best and Highest for All

Were these principles founded on new concepts I created myself? No, as you can see, they resemble timeless Truths taught throughout the ages. Therefore, they are nothing new in concept, yet they were creatively calibrated and organized to expedite great change.

Two months later, the principles' remarkable effects accelerated my mission exponentially. Not only were they transforming my life experience, but they were equally doing the same for others. The feedback was that their lives were more peaceful, manageable, and they loved what the principles were gifting them. This knowledge inspired me to teach workshops, which favorably demonstrated the effectiveness of this way to peace.

Confident in their abilities, in the spring of 2016, I decided it was time for the principles to make their way into the world. I would accomplish this by penning and publishing my first book.

This was an exciting time in my life because I finally felt secure in the stability of my calling. I had survived the launching of my mission, mapped and tracked the Truths Humanity needed, and created *a Daily Practice for Peace*. Additionally, I was well on my way to formulating the *Awakening Plan* for the advancement of Humanity's Awakening.

Life was grand!

Then, right as I was settling into the comfort of a routine I adored, everything changed again; not my mission's goals or another conscious expansion, but rather my location. This happened when I was told to move from the Cascade Mountains of Oregon to the Appalachian Mountains of North Georgia.

"Told?" Yes, *told*, via guidance given from beyond the veil. I know, for most adults *doing as told* is an odd concept, yet it is how I prefer living. It simplifies my life experience while navigating these foreign lands. It also guarantees I serve efficiently, which is vital with all I am on Earth to accomplish. Trust me, doing as *told* is worth its weight in gold when serving within Humanity's realm.

After heeding the call to relocate, I left Oregon in June. I drove a U-Haul, while my bestie Rachel drove my car on a 2,600-mile expedition. Why was I told to move? Truthfully, I do not know because I am not in the habit of asking "why" when *told* to do something. In my opinion, asking why is a waste of time since doing as told has never failed me.

Though I did not question the suggestion to move, years later, I figured it out. I was sent to Georgia because it was a more favorable place to live while founding the *Awakening Plan for Peace*. It is a location capable of providing me with the peace and ease I needed. After all, there is nothing like living amongst the sweet, soothing kindness of Southerners while assisting with seeing to the wellbeing of Humanity.

After settling in, with my mission now taking precedence over everything else, I dove headfirst back into my calling. Six months later, by wintertime, I was on target to publish my first book. It was a *How-To* book on achieving peace. Things were going well, better than expected! That is until the day came when fear and I collided—which entirely knocked my quest off its axis.

Our conflict started because fear was now aware of my ultimate intention: end its reign on Planet Earth. Is ending fear's rule even possible? It is! That is why it did not waste a single second launching its campaign against me. How did fear go about that? Sneakily, by getting someone else to do its dirty work.

Wait a minute… fear instructed someone else to act on its behalf? No. Instead, it filled them with worry over what they might lose if my mission progressed. It had them believing their calling on Earth would lose its significance. Then, because they thought it was true, they proceeded to stop my forward progression.

What happened exactly? That I will not disclose because I do not tell stories about the past—especially those playing the blame game since they relaunch drama and emotional mayhem.

What I can share, though, is I was devastated by the outcome of that person's actions because they deliberately placed question marks around the intentions of how I and others are serving. The result was that they planted seeds of doubt in the minds of their readers as to whether we and our teachings were trustworthy.

Though not telling stories is the stance I take, I will disclose the incredible toll the event took on me. I felt crushed, defeated, and unsure of how to proceed. I even wondered if the incident indicated it was not time for me to present what I was here to deliver. Maybe Humanity was not ready? Questioning our purpose highlighted this, which confused me because Humanity incessantly calls out for help and tirelessly pleads for assistance. Nevertheless, I could not help questioning if my purpose was unimportant. Maybe their ability to receive was delayed? Then, because I even questioned these things, help arrived immediately.

Chapter 3

An Intervention and Perceived Defeat

It was late December, shortly after fear had approached... when without notice, introduction, or a knock at the door, I turned to see a magnificent, illumined being enter my home. She was regal, knowing, and *of the Light,* the same *Light* I am familiar with beyond Humanity's realm.

Was she an Angel who served from afar? She was not. Instead, she was a highly evolved Truth-Seeker, who I will forever call my *Angel of saving grace.* Surprised by her visit and unable to speak, I gazed in awe while she stated her needs.

"Please give me the *Truth, Clarity, and Hope* I seek, so I can help Humanity return to peace. Share the *whole story,* the *big picture,* too, so I can understand our Truths and help them awaken. It's my calling, my quest, what I am here to do… and if you don't proceed with your mission, I'm unable to continue."

Showing her deep concern, she reached out, touched the heart of my soul, and pointedly asked, "Who are we? What are we? What else exists? Please answer our unanswered questions, so we can continue to exist."

Chills spiked my entire existence, and my wide-eyed response was, "Of course, I'll do as you ask. After all, it is my mission, calling, and quest."

She then left as abruptly as she had arrived, not even saying farewell. That was it, the extent of our first connection. Though her visit was brief, I knew what it meant; someone cared enough to help me get my mission back on track. And though she first appeared as her highest self in consciousness… I now know the being who came to save the day was my dearest, beloved Gail.

In the end, my perceived defeat was of no consequence. Instead, it was a gift and a defining moment… as nothing in my existence happens without a higher purpose. What was the gift? I realized something incredible: I was to go Big, rather than small, and get the *Awakening Plan for Peace* completed and delivered immediately!

With a new urgency and an understanding that Humanity was ready, I got straight to work. I worked every waking minute of each day, squeezing every second I could out of each of those days. I made phenomenal progress. In less than a week, I completed the strategic approach I would take to accomplish what she had asked. With all founding components mapped and tracked, I spent the next two months formulating everything needed to facilitate peace. By March (in less than three months) I had documented every Truth and step needed to help Humanity awaken.

I was thrilled for its completion! I was also excited because I already had a very successful collaborative partnership in place. This was a mandated requirement from beyond, a term of my calling so the *Awakening Plan* could publish on Earth.

My partner and I met in 2015, and as our relationship progressed, our callings united. She supported and assisted me throughout the entire process, and we both anxiously awaited this day. Once I completed all needed, we finalized our approach to launch and teach *how to ascend in consciousness.*

It was an exciting time for us both because we would finally fulfill what we desired most: help all who desired to waken, awaken. From there, together, we would assist with the restoration of peace on Earth.

Thank goodness I could finally breathe… with my quest officially back on track.

There was one problem, though. Amidst our excitement, I had completely forgotten about fear and its agenda. Unfortunately, fear had not forgotten about me. In fact, while my partner and I prepared to proceed, it found a new way to stop my forward momentum. This happened when fear destroyed our collaboration, which removed one of the people I most love on Earth from my life.

How did fear accomplish that? It found its own collaborator. Then, it pressed that person to do its dirty work just like it had before. That is the only detail I will share since, as stated previously, I refuse to tell stories that reopen doors of pain. What I can disclose, though, was the door between us closed and locked with no sign of it opening ever again. To this day, even with writing only a fraction of what happened, my entire existence still aches deeply. After all, it was one of the greatest losses I have ever experienced.

It was now April, and fear had managed to shut down my quest once again. Tragic? I no longer had the required partnership for the *Awakening Plan* to land, so yes. Equally unfortunate because I had lost the one I loved and the perfected match we were. Heartbroken and unsure what to do, I reached out to the beyond and requested a meeting with whom always knows best.

With an agreement to meet, I headed for a destination beyond the veil. My hope was I would benefit from the peace of mind my visit would bring. When I arrived, I was graciously received, and then I took a seat at the table where I usually sat. After giving me a moment to settle, I received condolences for the loss of my partner. Humanity's loss was sympathized too because the way to peace I was delivering was indefinitely delayed. With courtesies conveyed, I was asked if I had come to request a change in the terms of my calling.

"Of course not," I replied, surprised by the question. "I would never ask you to concede. Not only out of reverence but also because you know and see what's best for all. I'm grateful for the terms and conditions of my calling, as without them I would not have survived the tumultuous conditions on Earth."

"Then why do you visit?"

"Because of this," I pointed to my grieving heart. "And because I'm being pressed for the *Awakening Plan's* delivery. The Mortal Majority's fears are cresting because fear rules the hearts and minds of their beloveds."

"Your heart's condition is already known, and the urgency for the *Awakening Plan's* delivery is understood. Yet, there is little that can be offered other than condolences."

"I know," I whispered, while lowering my head onto my arms, which were resting on the table. I then inhaled deeply and released my sorrow in a flood of tears... not only for what I had lost but also for what Humanity must endure on Earth.

When I was complete, I leaned into the comfort of those present, which nearly lulled me to sleep. After what must have seemed like an eternity, I lifted my head and said, "I guess I'll be on my way."

A nod was all I received.

Then, as I turned to leave, I heard, "You'll need to form another collaboration before you can deliver Humanity's Truths and a way to awaken."

I nodded in acknowledgment.

"And," it was added, "to make sure the terms and conditions are clear, let's review them before you leave."

I agreed and sat again to receive them.

"First, your mission is to gather, map, organize, and deliver an *Awakening Plan for Peace* to Humanity. Do you have questions regarding this?"

"No, my mission's quite clear. Everything's complete except for the delivery."

"Perfect. Second, for this plan to see the light of day on Earth, a member of Humanity must step in with the desire to receive it. Additionally, they must collaborate with you on Humanity's behalf. The reason for this is, if one does not step in with a great desire to receive these gifts, then everything gifted will lose its value and validity. Which means, the plan's abilities would diminish significantly. Are we clear?"

"Yes. And please know, I'd do nothing to compromise the success of what I'm delivering."

"Third, you and your collaborative partner must never bring your personal beliefs into the equation. The reason for this is, belief discrepancies propagate contempt on Planet Earth. Questions?"

"No, I clearly understand."

"Fourth, the one who steps in to collaborate must be a veiled human living on Earth. The reason for this is, it's from their experiences and understandings that Humanity can most effectively waken. After all, with how you exist in consciousness, you'll not easily understand the hurdles most encounter. With this condition met, the collaboration between your veiled partner and yourself in consciousness will have every aspect covered. In conclusion, these are the terms you must adhere to while serving within their lands."

"Understood," I answered.

Though the purpose of my visit had concluded, I lingered longer for additional comfort. When complete, I expressed my appreciation and then reluctantly headed back to my home on Earth.

After returning, the comfort I had gleaned from beyond quickly faded, as I again felt Humanity pressing for a way to peace. I had no idea what to do since fear was tracking my every move and aiming at those I loved. What I did know, though, was that it was unacceptable for me to knowingly subject anyone to fear's destruction. After all, it was obvious fear's issue was only with me. With that knowing, and realizing fear was determined to end my quest, I decided that suspending my mission was the only way I could ensure its preservation.

Exhausted and confused, I bolted all doors into my world and isolated myself. Did I leave a way in, just in case someone could help? No. With my worries building and feeling defeated, it never crossed my mind. Though my intent was for all collaborative possibilities to cease, in the end, a miracle masterfully navigated her way back into my life. This was so she could fulfill her earthbound mission: to retrieve Humanity's highest Truths and a way to awaken, for the achievement of peace on Earth.

Chapter 4

Hide, Seek, Found, and Called Out

Two months after I had closed all doors into my world, there I sat on my living room floor, commiserating my mission's shutdown. I had surrounded myself with the piles of content contributing to the *Awakening Plan's* completion, hoping to find solace amongst it all. It helped because Truth is what comforts me the most. Yet, I worried if everything was useless now, with its purpose blocked by fear and its agenda.

Feeling lost, I questioned why this was the situation in which I found myself. I had given my all, done my best, and readied everything precisely as Humanity had asked. Nevertheless, to no avail, I was failing my earthly calling. With no hope in sight, I began preparing myself for a final grade of *Mission Incomplete.* Then, just as I was on the edge of giving up and conceding it all as a loss… my *Angel of saving grace* showed herself again. This time, though, she presented as a version of her earthly existence.

Gail arrived as she had before, without notice or introduction. She blew in like a mighty wind… swift, targeted, and calculated. Wasting not a single second, she announced she would not allow my choices to compromise her calling. Surprised, I informed her that my home and I were in no condition for her unannounced visit. She waved me off, saying our condition was of no concern because she needed to speak to me immediately.

Knowing who she was, and with my curiosity rising, I asked, "What about?"

"The Truths you found," she answered. "I was told you tracked Humanity's highest, and you have them in your possession. I was also told you have detailed instructions for how Humanity can ascend in consciousness. I need those now so I can advance their Awakening."

She then became quiet, chewed on her lip, and studied me intently.

"That was straight to the point," I thought to myself, which had my heart hanging on her every word. I then felt a glimmer of hope because she was seeking the *Awakening Plan for Peace* specifically. Maybe she saw a clear path for herself to receive it on Humanity's behalf? If that was her intent, then I could meet the terms of my mission. With these possibilities quickly unfolding, I felt an immediate lessening of the load I had been carrying.

"Well…" Gail interrupted my thoughts, "is what I was told true?"

Realizing she was waiting for my answer, I gave her an exaggerated, slow nod of yes.

With my confirmation, she appeared to relax, which led us into a moment of silence. During our pause, I could tell Gail was collecting her thoughts and trying to take it all in. On the other hand, I was attempting to center myself while drifting in and out of disbelief that collaboration was within reach. After taking the time she required, she leaned toward me and stated her needs.

"Please tell me the Truths you know, and please explain why we on Earth must continue facing the pain we do. Why must we suffer? Why is it allowed to continue? Is there a way for us to rise out of it all? If so, give me the *Truth* and *Clarity* I need so that *Hope* can comfort us all."

She paused, leaned in closer, fascinating the heart of my soul with her gaze. When she knew she had my attention, she whispered, "Please hide no more, please don't hold back, please tell me all you know."

My eyes widened, I shivered to the core of my existence, and I uttered an inaudible "Wow…" to myself. First, for the impact of her line of questioning, then because she had called me out. Needing a moment, I took time to piece together what this all meant. Simply stated, what it meant was, I needed to consider stepping back into my mission. When I emerged from my thoughts, I noticed Gail was waiting for me to speak. Now, though, I had no idea what to say.

"Well…" she prompted. "Why are you hiding?"

Shaking my head at the enormity of it all, I answered her question the best I could.

"I've gone into hiding for a couple of reasons. First, I needed a break from fear's ongoing attempts to end my quest. Second, I had to shut things down to protect the viability of my mission. Otherwise, I may have lost the opportunity to fulfill it. Last…" I reluctantly shared the memory of that day, "I needed time for my heart to mend."

Gail stared at me while her expression shifted several times. "Your heart needs to mend? That makes no sense with how you were created."

"Maybe it doesn't, but don't overlook the fact I'm currently serving in a body with an *earthly heart*," I highlighted, not understanding why so many people were confused that I felt things deeply too. Not wanting to park on that ongoing mystery, I pressed forward.

"And, Gail, you asked why?"

She nodded.

"It's because I lost one of the people I love most. She partnered with me to help Humanity awaken with the means and way to the peace you are seeking. Then, right before we launched our intent, we were told we had to part ways. And ever since we said our goodbyes… I've not been allowed to see her again. Hence, my heart needed mending."

She sat quietly, listening, so I continued.

"And, so you know, Gail, I wouldn't call my reprieve 'hiding.' Instead, I'd call it retreating to mindfully assess that failed attempt. Because, ultimately, all outcomes are of my responsibility."

After my explanation was complete, I quieted myself to avoid an emotional meltdown with my heart still grieving. I then gazed out the window, which led us both to a mutually imposed time out.

After many minutes, I asked, "Do you understand why I needed a break? Why I withdrew?"

"Yes," she whispered, "it's because fear took someone you love from you and ended your opportunity to fulfill your quest."

"Exactly." I bit my lip, holding back my tears.

After thoughtful contemplation, Gail said, "You've opened the door to me today. Will you at least consider ending your retreat? I know what happened was difficult, yet I equally know how dire the conditions on Earth are. How important it is we get Humanity a way to peace immediately."

Though she pulled my calling's heartstrings, she did not understand the complexities of her request. First, there were the terms and conditions of my calling, which we would have to meet. I shared them with her and explained that unless they were satisfied, we could not deliver what she had come to retrieve.

Then there was the issue of fear itself, as it might wreak havoc in her life if she partnered with me. It was a risk that she would need to consider since fear will do everything to maintain its rule. I confessed if it interfered again, I was unsure I would survive another undoing like the last. After sharing the need for her thoughtful consideration, she came and sat before me. Kindly taking my hands into hers, she said the following.

"I see the full scope of it all, you know I do. The fact is, the time has come for us to help. Please come out of hiding and collaborate. I am not at odds with fear, nor prone to it toppling me. And," she squeezed my hands, "I'm more than ready to receive."

I exhaled deeply, contemplating my readiness to risk it all again. I questioned my ability to survive a loss like the last, knowing it could have me sinking into a hopeless abyss. I knew moving forward with Gail was the best and highest for all. Yet, I was uncertain I had recovered enough to endure the amount of work it would place on me.

I had to consider the physical toll on my body due to the massive amount of energy these collaborations take. I not only had to contend with what fear threw my way, but I also had to help my partner with fear's consequences. Those are heavy loads to carry, and I often carried the bulk of the weight for us both.

Still uncertain, I evaluated the Truth-Seeker sitting before me. I perceived nothing other than her love, dedication, and determination for Humanity. I also clearly saw that she was qualified to receive all I was delivering. With new clarity, I knew I needed to consider ending my time of reprieve.

"I'm up to the task," she locked eyes with me, "and I promise if you step into a collaborative quest with me, I'll see it through to completion. I believe we can conquer fear together! I know it's possible, I know it's true."

I slowly nodded an acknowledgment. Then, I thoughtfully contemplated Gail's offer since she had the ability to see this through better than anyone else. When complete, I inhaled deeply and announced, "I'll hide no more."

"Does this mean we can work together? You'll collaborate with me?" Gail's eyes brightened while she fidgeted.

"I'll come out of hiding to spend time with you..." I smiled at her heartwarming persistence. "Then, I'll consider giving collaboration another chance."

"Thank you, thank you, thank you!" She stood and raised her arms to the sky. "Can we start today? Because I'm ready to receive."

"Mmm..." I considered, since her enthusiasm was likely the medicine I needed.

"Please..." She pressed her palms together.

"Yes, we can begin today," I finally agreed, knowing leaving the house would benefit me. "Let's meet at a restaurant because I need to eat. And while we're there, I can share a dose of the *Truth, Clarity, and Hope* you asked to receive."

This offer catapulted her to the moon and beyond, which thankfully boosted my consideration to give collaboration another chance.

Chapter 5

First Dose of Truth, Clarity, and Hope

When I entered the restaurant, I found Gail sitting in a corner booth at the far end of the room, giving us the privacy I desired. She welcomed me with a giant smile and said she was grateful we could start today. She explained it would benefit her preparations for our upcoming collaborative endeavor. Though I found her statement presumptuous since I had not agreed to collaborate yet, I just grinned and sat at the table across from where she was sitting.

Gail then eagerly announced she would like to use our time together to ask a few basic questions. She would then use the answers to develop a more thorough, in-depth line of questioning. Gail thought this would have all I am here to deliver landing linearly for ease of comprehension. She then assured me she would get to work immediately. When complete, her summed inquiries would be known as her official *Q and A*.

I thanked her in advance for her efforts and took a quick look at the menu as the waiter approached. After ordering, Gail and I quickly dropped into her unscripted questions. Her first queries were the usual most people ask: the whats, whys, and hows. What is going on in the world? Why is Humanity not living in peace? How do we get ourselves out of this mess?

Warmed with her curiosities and ramblings, I easily slid into our discussion.

"Okay, Gail," I began, "let's discuss *'Why is Humanity not living in peace?'* first. In short, they're not living in peace because of their Second Intention. However, their core issues stem from the terms they requested within that intention."

Gail tilted her head. "Second Intention?"

"Yes, Humanity's Second Intention. It came into play when they wanted to have their earthly experience, and all future endeavors come from their efforts and determinations only. Summed, Humanity asked they be given 'sole authority' to govern over all happenings on Planet Earth."

"What are you talking about?" Her eyes widened.

Knowing there was likely another question to follow, I waited for her next.

Several moments later, she said, "Details please, especially regarding the 'terms' you mentioned."

"Sure. Humanity's terms were to be given *free will* and for there to be *no Divine intervention* after the sanctioning of their Second Intention. Then, to make sure their new life experience advanced as desired, they veiled themselves. Meaning, they put a permanent barrier between themselves, the Divine, and all necessary resources beyond their existence."

Gail's eyes expanded even further as her mouth dropped open.

Knowing this was all unrelatable to her understanding, because of how she served, I asked, "Are you okay?"

"I'm not sure." She closed her eyes while rocking her head side to side. When she reopened them, she asked, "Humanity intentionally separated themselves from the Divine? Who would choose that? It doesn't make sense."

"I know." I sighed, remembering my shock from discovering this Truth. The moment when I saw Humanity deliberately untying themselves from all existing beyond their world. I felt devastated, and the event was so unnerving it took months for me to recover.

Interrupting my thoughts, Gail asked, "Why was their Second Intention granted?"

"It was granted because Humanity pressed and insisted that their terms be met until they were. And trust me, Gail," I emphasized, "the one who agreed to *free will* and *no Divine intervention* did so with great reluctance."

"What about the veiling?"

"It was an afterthought, not a sanctioned term or an arranged agreement. It was a choice Humanity made for themselves. Over time, due to this choice, they came to live as they do today... unawakened, within The Illusion, and with fear ruling on Planet Earth.

"The veil is also why," I continued, "wars, violence, racism, hate, poverty, pain, and suffering exist. Additionally, it's why many on Earth now believe the Divine no longer cares about them or their wellbeing."

Gail sat in silence, wearing an expression of disbelief. I pulled back, allowing her time to adapt to the disclosures. Several moments later, I asked again, "Are you okay?"

"I'm just confused…" She blinked several times. "So basically, you're saying all ailing Humanity resulted from their Second Intention? That their intention was grievous from its beginning?"

"Not quite," I replied, shaking my head. "Instead, I would say their Second Intention was well-considered and filled with amazing possibilities. Yet, Humanity's choice to veil was the demise of all they desired to achieve."

"The demise?" she asked.

"Yes, the demise. Because when Humanity put their Second Intention in motion, all that was most meaningful to them was compromised, including the goals they set within their First Intention. Which…"

"Hold on." Gail stopped me midsentence. "These Truths deeply resonate within me, but my mind needs help organizing them."

Knowing what would provide clarity, I suggested I introduce her to Humanity's Three Intentions. With her agreement, I pulled a sheet of paper from my back pocket and set it on the table. "Here you go. These are all the intentions Humanity has set as of today."

Gail leaned in to review the document.

HUMANITY'S THREE INTENTIONS

FIRST INTENTION

To Exist in Yet Another Way

Goal of the First Intention: establish an additional, unique life experience exclusive unto themselves. To be created, filled, and fashioned with what they wanted most: love, joy, peace, and endless explorations.

SECOND INTENTION

To Exist To Their Fullest Potential

Goal of the Second Intention: experience themselves entirely as the creative beings they were created to be.

The Terms	The After Thought
Free Will	A Self-Imposed Veiling
No Divine Intervention	

THIRD INTENTION

To Exist in Consciousness Again

Goal of the Third Intention: collectively awaken, for the achievement of peace on Earth.

(Dear Reader: visit *www.MyCallingMyQuest.com* to download a more readable illustration in a free PDF format. This includes all handouts within this book.)

After she finished reading, Gail looked at me and uttered, "Wow… these are incredible."

"Right?" I smiled. "Can you see the demise in it all now?"

"Not really." She looked to the handout again. "Can you tell me?"

"Absolutely. The issue with Humanity's Second Intention was that it inadvertently compromised their first. Most notably, their ability to live in joy, love, and peace."

"Got it. Their Second intention took that all away. And," she added, "that's probably why Humanity set their Third Intention."

"It is!" I excited for her excellent deduction.

Reviewing the intentions again, Gail muttered, "The Third Intention…" Then she looked at me and enthused, "The day the decision was made!"

"How do you know about that?" I laughed, enjoying where her Truth-Seeking curiosities had taken her.

"I read the piece you wrote that was published in 2015. I found it when I was tracking your achievements before I came to call you out. I wanted to see if the Truths you're here to share had landed. What you wrote was an amazing read, but it didn't contain what I was searching for."

"Correct, it did not, since that was written to check Humanity's receptivity to their Truths."

"Did you get a response?"

"Just you!"

Frowning, she asked, "How can that be? It inspired me to find you."

"It's Truth." I shrugged one shoulder. "It either grabs ahold of someone's heart and inspires them or goes over their head as though it was never said."

"I don't understand." Gail's brow tightened. "What you shared was a complete disclosure about the actual day Humanity decided to awaken. You let everyone on Earth know they are loved and that multitudes of souls are coming to help."

"That's true, but what did you expect?" I asked, unsure of her point.

"I expected those who read it to engage with their Truths. And honestly, I'm disappointed no one has contacted you to discuss what happened."

Her reaction concerned me, so I searched to see why she'd had it. When I found the issue, I explained how we would need to proceed.

"Gail, if we're going to step into a collaborative effort to help Humanity, you'll need to manage your expectations. Otherwise, you're setting yourself up for disappointment. After all, there's a possibility this way to peace may not get used at all."

"Seriously? It may not get used?" She tensed.

"It may not," I shrugged again, "that's a reality I had to accept myself."

"Then how can you continue serving while knowing this? And I don't understand why they would ask for a plan to awaken and not use it."

Realizing she was not making the connection, I spoke to her concerns.

"First, I'm able to continue serving because my commitment is not hinged on expectations of a particular outcome. Second, regarding your worries about Humanity using a plan to awaken or not, you're forgetting that those who requested its delivery will put it to use."

"I'm confused." She squinted. "Who asked for Humanity's Truths and a way to awaken?"

"The Mortal Majority, the souls of Humanity."

"It was only their souls?"

"In conscious agreement, yes. Sure, humankind wants to achieve peace, yet it was their souls who called for their collective Awakening."

Gail dropped her head, swayed it back and forth, and then looked up. "I thought I was ready for this, and I thought I would easily grasp what you're here to share. Why's this so difficult for me to understand?"

"There are a couple of reasons. The first is because you're not remembering that you are only one part of your total self. This is true for everyone living this side of the veil. We'll discuss that when I provide the clarity you came to receive.

"Also," I continued, "you're having difficulties because conditions on Earth are greatly impacting your ability to recall higher Truths."

"But I've worked with some of the highest Truths, so why are these so difficult for me to wrap my mind around?"

"It's because I'm sharing Truths that originated from the beginning of everyone's existence. Therefore, many of them are beyond your reach, so go easy on yourself." I patted her hand.

Gail sighed, then said, "You have no difficulties with these Truths, and the conditions here don't seem to affect you. What's the difference between you and me?"

I softly chuckled, wondering how she would respond to my answer. "The difference is, you're veiled, and I'm not."

"Wow…" Gail went starry-eyed, showing she understood unveiled indicated I was fully conscious.

Shaking my head with knowing the reason for her reaction, I said, "Gail, living this way is not so exceptional. After all, I only exist on Earth like everyone would if Humanity had not veiled."

"Mmm…" she grinned, "I disagree with you completely. Living unveiled is impressive! Especially if it gives you the ability to discover and deliver Humanity's highest Truths. Therefore, I'm holding to it's quite exceptional."

"Okay…" I raised my hands, conceding, "I'll agree with you to some degree, since I am exceptionally *You* before you were veiled, and I experience consciousness as Humanity once did. Also," I emphasized, "I represent how everyone can live on Earth again."

Gail scooted to the edge of her seat, leaning into what I had shared. "Everyone can live unveiled on Earth?"

"Yes, after they awaken."

"Incredible…" she murmured to herself. Then she asked, "What's it like to live on Earth this way?"

"Well, that would take days to explain," I laughed. "So, let's save that discussion for another time."

"Just an example, please?"

"All right…" I gave in. "It's enchanting, fantastical, unimaginable, bizarre, confusing, difficult, on the edge of sanity, and nearly impossible to believe it's true," I laughed, with how crazy it all sounded.

"You know," I looked directly at Gail, "the sanity part was the most difficult to manage since I was not given a road map, guide, or teacher to navigate my consciousness. In the end, though," I smiled, happy for it, "I think it's miraculous I figured out how to survive it all!"

"So, how does living this way apply to your experience on Earth?"

"Hmm…" I paused, unsure of how to answer. "Give me a moment to think about how to explain that."

Gail agreed and started reading Humanity's intentions again.

After a couple of minutes, I resumed. "Okay, here's how living unveiled applies to my experience on Earth. I'm not bound by the veil Humanity placed. I can see what's happening beyond Humanity's existence. I can track and map the Truths Humanity is seeking back to the place where no one exists. I can share those Truths on Earth directly, not as an intermediary. I have real-time interactions with others who are not a part of Humanity's collective. Meaning, I consciously have life experiences here, *There*, and beyond simultaneously," I concluded, with a wink.

"That's amazing!"

"And, there's more…" I lingered, knowing she would love this. "Not only do I have life experiences beyond the veil, but I also consciously work daily on Humanity's behalf here and *There*."

"You work on Earth and *There* simultaneously?" Gail's jaw dropped.

"I do. In fact," I chimed, having fun with the topic, "you can add working in the beyond to the list."

"Well then," she laughed, "that explains why living unveiled is not significant to you. Because working here, *There*, and beyond trumps that!"

"Right?" I laughed with her. "And know serving in all these locations at the same time is significant to me too."

"How many others have you met on Earth who live this way?"

"Only one, the person I collaborated with last. We frequently worked together here and *There*. It was the most awesome, outrageous experience I've had while serving on Earth."

"Wow…" she trailed off, possibly trying to imagine living this way.

I could tell from her expression she was daydreaming, so I decided to use the opportunity to eat my meal before she asked a new question. After I finished, I interrupted her thoughts. "Do you have any other questions that will help with the development of your *Q and A*?"

"I do. Why do you believe everything I've come to receive can accomplish Humanity's Awakening and return to peace?"

"That's simple. I believe it because everything I'm here to deliver will provide a solution for the number one unsolved problem on Planet Earth."

"And that problem is?"

"Despite Humanity's insatiable desire to live in harmony, they lack any plan or collaborative effort to get them to their desired destination, peace on Earth."

"And the solution is?"

"First, Humanity needs to make peace their highest priority. Then, they need to agree on and implement a means and way to peace. Something like the *Awakening Plan for Peace* and the Truths revealed within it."

"The plan has a name?" Gail asked excitedly.

"It does! And it also has the ability to get Humanity to peace."

"Tell me more, please… Like what aspect of the *Awakening Plan* will help Humanity most?"

"Well…" I paused, considering, "I'd say Truth will help the most, via the account of Humanity's existence. Because it addresses the pressing questions that many have. In particular, the *Whys*. Like, why does Humanity live as they do? Why does violence, poverty, racism, hate, and intolerance continue, despite everyone wanting them to end?

"You see," I continued, "it's believed for Humanity to embrace a way to awaken, they'll need their questions answered first. So, the Truths found within this *Awakening Plan* are a great choice to address their *Whys*."

"We definitely have a whole lot of *Whys* on Earth right now. Can you share more about what's included?"

"Absolutely. Summed, aside from Truth, this *Awakening Plan* provides clarity regarding how Humanity descended in consciousness. It also includes tools and solutions from which they can launch their Awakening. After they master their conscious ascent, there are instructions on how they can help others awaken. Then, when enough people have transcended fear and separation, there are suggestions for how to collaborate to live in peace globally."

"Imagine that…" Gail looked away, taking a moment to consider the day everyone would live on Earth in unified harmony. When complete, she asked why I was certain Humanity could pull off a collective Awakening.

I smiled confidently before answering. "There are many reasons why I know they can pull this off. First, just look around you and see everything Humanity's capable of when they put their hearts, minds, and passionate creativity to use. My goodness, what they've established throughout their time on Earth is amazing! People forget to recognize and acknowledge their brilliance."

"Okay, I hear you. Yet, currently, the total of Humanity isn't effectively working together to achieve peace."

"True, yet there's great hope regarding their issues with global collaboration as well."

"Seriously? What magician's hat do you think that miracle will get pulled from?" She teasingly mocked.

Ignoring her cynicism, I answered, "It's a miracle that's already happened. Or, shall I say, has already landed."

"What are you talking about?"

"I'm talking about a group of people who are already working together. Those who have existing intentions of seeing to the welfare of everyone and everything existing on Earth. In fact," I emphasized, "they are the primary reason Humanity may accomplish a collective Awakening. Make no mistake about it, Gail, these people have no issue with collaboration for the benefit of all."

"The Truth-Seekers?"

"Nope," I quipped, "try again."

"Hmm…" Gail looked around the room, then laughed when she made the connection. "The Millennials! The cause-driven, change-making generation who can raise global consciousness greater than most."

"Exactly. And know if anyone on Earth can help lead Humanity to a peaceful, awakened experience, it is this generation and likely those who follow."

"That makes sense," she nodded. "And their efforts combined with ours has me considering peace on Earth as a possibility too. Thank you for the clarity, it's benefited my perspective."

"You're welcome."

I then paid the bill and let her know it was time to part ways for the day. Once outside, she asked if there was anything else of importance she needed to know. I took a moment to review what we had discussed and shared that there was one item of great importance. It was something she would need to accomplish if we were to collaborate. Specifically, she must release all expectations regarding the outcomes of our efforts.

This surrender needed to include how Humanity received the *Awakening Plan for Peace*. Because if the only result of what we shared were hearts, minds, and dialogues amongst Humanity opening, then all that we presented would serve an astounding purpose.

Gail agreed to the terms and confirmed she would comply with my request. I thanked her and asked if she had any other questions. With a warm smile, sparkling eyes, and wide-open heart, she leaned in close and asked, "Will you please agree to collaborate with me?"

I smiled, knowing it was foolish to forgo this outstanding opportunity. She had proven her deep love and dedication to Humanity and understood their needs better than most. Though I was not prepared to say yes so soon, I leaned my heart into hers and whispered, "Yes, dear Gail, I am willing to collaborate with you."

Thrilled with my agreement, she asked if we could meet in five weeks, allowing her time to develop her official *Q and A*. I readily agreed, with a month affording me ample time to clean up my home, life, and emotional wellbeing. This was necessary, so I could give this incredible collaborative opportunity the best I have ever given.

After arriving home, I decided to go on a fact-finding search to investigate our previous points of connection. Whether Gail recalled it or not, this was not the first time we had crossed paths.

Why investigate? First, I wanted to increase my limited knowledge of her. My investigation was similar to completing a background check, a responsible thing to do before commencing any working relationship. I also wanted to prepare for Gail's questions regarding her entire existence, which would arise from her insatiable curiosity. Additionally, I had a deep desire to know if we were destined for success in our collaborative quest. If it looked problematic, at least I would gain awareness of the potential hurdles we could face.

Last, in all honesty, I sought peace of mind to ensure our collaboration would benefit us both. After all, due to the perspective I have, I am personally responsible for our mutual wellbeing, which meant that though I had given a yes, if proceeding was not the best and highest for all, we would need to consider an alternative agreement.

Chapter 6

The Truth-Seekers

When I landed where I could gather the information I sought, I was immediately flooded with *the Light* that had shaped the realm where Gail was from. Was it necessary to visit here to track our first point of connection? Absolutely not, but why wouldn't I? Since this location was a welcomed reprieve from the conditions existing on Earth.

Settling in, I reminded myself I needed to visit this realm more frequently, with its abilities to nurture one's wellbeing greater than anywhere within the multi-realm Universe. Basking in its peacefulness, I acknowledged feeling guilty about preferring this realm's comforts over my home of origin. I loved my home in the realm of Truth, but this was the place I preferred when needing rest and relaxation.

Are there differences between the two realms? Yes, many! Most notable, their energetic composition and intentions, which affect souls' desires to visit one over the other. For instance, the realm of Truth is composed of Truth only, which for some feels cold and uninviting, causing visitors to retreat quickly. Others have implied the realm of Truth is boring, which places it low on the list of destinations to visit.

This choice I understand, since it is an all work, little play, business-comes-first dimension. Know, though, this arrangement is imperative because it is the primary realm supporting *All that Exists*. I liken it to *Mission Control* at NASA, where a team of highly focused people is seeing to the wellbeing of all who rely on them.

Sounds intense, right? It is!

What about this realm? The home of those who assist with the wellbeing of all existing?

Well, it's beyond dreamy…

Understand, *dreamy* is not my opinion only, with souls voting this realm as their favored destination. These accolades are unanimously maintained since its composition is comprised *of the Light* and love only. Though this realm ranks highest in places to visit, it rates even higher in its purpose, because the only calling those residing here seek is to tend to those in need of assistance. In fact, their agendas are never about themselves or their desires.

Though true, serving is not their only point of connection because their personal relationships are of great importance too. Their relationships are some of the most Divine and purposeful partnerships I have ever experienced. This is why those from here are a phenomenal choice to help Humanity awaken—since they live in the same fashion Humanity desires to exist.

With my current vantage point, I might as well answer a question many have asked: How can you identify a soul from this realm while they are working on Planet Earth? You will know in how they serve because they seek only one purpose: to be the way-showers to all higher consciousness.

You will also know in how they live, as their mission takes precedence over all else. Additionally, they do not serve for personal gain or have agendas other than their callings. That is where you will find the degree of differentiation. However, some may opt for personal gain currently because getting sidetracked and distracted on Earth is quite common.

Realizing I had sidetracked myself, I decided it was time to track the facts I had come to retrieve, hoping above all else to confirm Gail and I were well-matched to fulfill a mutual quest. With my intention set, I started at the very beginning, the same beginning where everything began… when one's desire rises to exist as soul.

Gail and I both incepted in the same way all souls do. The difference in how she and I came about versus others was we both consciously chose to exist in service. In fact, this was the choice that all Truth-Seekers make upon their creation. After making that decision, we located to where we were most needed. Initially, Gail and I served in two different dimensions. I in the realm of Truth, and she two dimensions away from my own—which indicated she had served on behalf *of the Light* exclusively from the moment of her soul's initiation. I, on the other hand, was only ever a member of *Team Truth*.

Does this signify the basis of my calling was different than Gail's? Yes. Not only in the origin of my creation but equally in my eternal service purpose. However, when I vowed to serve Humanity, those *of the Light* and I became one and the same. Shivering, I exhaled, relieved with my first validation; Gail and I were a verified collaborative match in our current service intentions. With that knowledge, I continued my investigation.

Eternities passed after our initial realm placements. Then the day came when I, Gail, and others were invited to consider a new service agreement. We were informed a new collaborative effort was quickly forming, with a realm beyond our Universe needing immediate assistance. A collective named Humanity had sent out the call, and they urgently needed to know if we could help. Gail and I answered, "Yes," which made this event our first point of connection.

After we agreed to assist, we were assigned to the dimension where Gail already lived. Initially, we were only allowed to serve Humanity from afar. Our job was to shower them with loving support until our service on Earth was permitted. When would that allowance be granted? The day when Humanity earnestly contemplated a collective Awakening. Serving in this way was a high honor, yet we anxiously awaited the day when we could fulfill our Earthly commission.

With everyone readying themselves to serve on Earth, some agreed to take on an additional task: seek the highest Truths of all and assimilate them on Humanity's behalf. This was when my expertise came into play, as primarily I am a Truth-Seeker—it is my specialty. I trained others in how to perform their duties, and when training was complete, they were known as Truth-Seekers just like me.

I am certain Gail and I must have crossed paths during this time, yet I do not recall meeting her during her schooling. Even so, I now clearly understood she had trained to serve like me. With this understanding, I now knew our current collaboration was set for success!

After Gail became a Truth-Seeker, and eons of non-time had passed, we were finally allowed to serve on Earth. Had Humanity decided to awaken? Not yet, but there was great hope that day was within reach. This prospect was enough for us to commence our earthly incarnations and ready ourselves for how we would serve next.

Feeling thrilled we were a collaborative match, I began examining our experiences on Earth, with hopes I would discover we were perfectly aligned there as well.

Chapter 7

Gail and I

Gail and I arrived on Planet Earth a decade apart. Was it predetermined we would serve together? It was a distinct possibility but not guaranteed. First, we would each need to learn how to navigate these lands with our faculties still intact. Meaning, we would both have to face intentional life experiences not easily endured so that we could gain understandings regarding what Humanity must contend with on Earth. What were our life experiences? Were we a paired match here too?

Here's the deal… I do not peek in on one's existence without permission. Therefore, I will only share what is commonly known about Gail. The first thing I know, undoubtedly, is Gail was veiled. She underwent the systematic, highly regimented domestication process most humans do when birthed on Earth.

What does that mean? It means she received an education in how to exist as a human. She was taught how to abide by Humanity's rules of engagement and schooled in how to comply with the code of ethics they collectively created. Therefore, she became a domesticated human being, which sealed the deal on her veiling.

Following this conditioning, typically completed between ages 2-4, Gail's childhood was riddled with experiences a child should never have to endure. Though true, know it was Gail herself who had authorized her difficulties. She sanctioned and orchestrated them so she could compassionately lead as intended when she came of age.

Though her childhood was difficult and filled with trials, as a young woman, Gail courageously found her way to a better life. Her first step to secure that was pursuing higher education. Next, she tapped into her Truth-Seeking abilities to find solutions for the difficulties she had experienced. This resulted in her gaining steady footing to heal emotionally and rise in consciousness. With those gains, she then pursued a career that paved the way for how she serves today—from a global platform.

Gail initially achieved that outstanding professional accomplishment by helping others to overcome their afflictions. She did this by sharing her expertise in how to move beyond the past emotionally, mentally, and spiritually. The result was that she helped many successfully break free from the fear, sorrow, and pain that had previously bound them. In time, after fine-tuning her Truth-Seeking abilities, she became a highly regarded *go-to* resource in how to awaken. She is now collaborating with other highly evolved Truth-Seekers, and together their focus is to help Humanity reach peace.

As I looked in on what Gail had achieved, I could not help feeling impressed with her success in reaching so many with Truth. It's quite remarkable how just one person can expedite significant change by committing their entirety to it. Despite what she has accomplished, she has never rested on her achievements. Nor has she ever given up on searching for the highest Truths, including the Truths found within the *Awakening Plan for Peace*.

How did Gail know this plan for peace existed? Her highest self in consciousness spoke of it, prompting her to search high and low to find the one who had it within her possession. With conditions as they were on Earth, Gail wasted not a single second pursuing what she believed would be her most promising collaboration. This, fortunately, led her to me.

On the flip side, my experience on Earth was both similar and different from Gail's. Similar, because I had also encountered complicated childhood experiences. These, in total, were pivotal to my understanding of what others faced. Different because, as mentioned, I came in unveiled. I then maintained that state of consciousness so I could fulfill my purpose: find, assimilate, and deliver Humanity's higher Truths.

What was it like living on Earth this way?

Honestly, it was difficult and filled with many complications. In my younger years, less so because I was rarely exposed to the world outside of my home. That all changed the day I started primary education. That event was when my difficulties here increased exponentially. How could they not, with having to figure out how to navigate this time and space place by myself? With having to endure wide-open, never-ending exposure to all existing beyond Humanity's realm?

In summation, living this way was precarious because there were *zero degrees of separation* in my all-inclusive conscious experience. The result was that I and others wondered if I had a peculiar form of "insanity," especially when I spoke of what I saw and knew. As a young child, I quickly learned not to talk of such things; this practice carried well into my thirties.

Though my mental wellness was frequently questioned, in my late twenties, I fortunately found ways to cope with my consciousness. This was essential; otherwise, I would never achieve a *Mission Complete*.

How did I find my way? First, I put my well-honed tracking skills to use and relentlessly searched for answers. Then, when I found solutions, I utilized them to experience higher degrees of emotional and mental wellbeing. Thankfully, my efforts paid off, gifting me greater peace than I had yet to experience while living on Earth.

After finding my way and acquiring greater understandings, I started assisting others who were facing similar conscious experiences—many of whom were rapidly Awakening. This work was important to me because people needed to know their rising consciousness was not a form of mental illness: an illness frequently misdiagnosed on Earth due to a lack of knowledge in how consciousness progresses.

This consideration puts a new spin on what mental illness is because, minus the exceptions, all it is in Truth is: varying degrees of awareness that fluctuate due to one's conscious or unconscious situation. Fluctuations that greatly impact one's conscious abilities by residing in a place that is filled with *endless contradictions*. For instance, *who everyone is or is not in Truth*.

Therefore, with these knowings, let's name mental illness for what it is: it is a state-of-consciousness people are navigating while living on Planet Earth. It is also a condition that sometimes requires assistance or a treatment plan to manage it. And please understand, I am not endorsing tossing all professional help and medication out the window with these insights because sometimes those are necessary too. Whether one agrees or disagrees, I am grateful I found a way to live in conscious stability.

Although, as we know, there are two sides to every scenario. Sure, I was experiencing greater ease with my new state of mind. Yet, with my new stability and awareness, I began regretting how my unveiled existence impacted others; most importantly, my family and friends who I had overly burdened with how I consciously existed. Though the difficulties I caused were unintentional, I have never shaken the guilt I carry from my actions. After finding my way, I performed better than I had. However, I still had huge learning curves to contend with since my consciousness continued affecting myself and those I loved.

Did I figure it out? Not entirely, but I did reach the place where I experienced greater peace and ease by my mid-thirties. That was followed by 13 more years of nearly the same. I cannot begin to explain how that period benefited my calling, as the quality of life I experienced was a welcomed reprieve. Equally, it was a beautiful gift because it afforded me the time I needed to gain stable footing before my highest mission on Earth launched in 2014.

So, were Gail and I compatible on Earth equally? After my thorough review, I would say absolutely! She may have some hurdles to overcome because she veiled, but it appeared there were relatively few. This meant there was a possibility of collaborative success here as well, especially with what we each brought to the table.

Gail's personal life experiences gave her the ability to lead in compassionate, effective ways. It also allowed her to help others navigate their Awakenings, despite the endless hurdles fear placed before them. Her established belief that life's gravest difficulties were resolvable provided others with the confidence they needed to rise above their pain and suffering.

For me, my life experiences afforded me the ability to help others navigate their risings in consciousness. That included addressing perceived mental illnesses and seizing solutions in how to live to their highest potential. In total, this meant that between the two of us, we had all bases covered to help guide Humanity through their collective Awakening. Hence, overall, we were a perfect match!

Completing my investigation, I headed back to Earth, gratified with finding the peace of mind I had sought. Her fear was low, her knowledge grand, and since she was a Truth-Seeker, she was trained to receive the Truths I was delivering. With newfound confidence in our compatibility tracked, I now knew committing to collaborate with Gail was the best choice I could have made. If fear tried to derail me again, I knew Gail and I were up to the challenge. I then realized that the *Awakening Plan's*

delivery was a real possibility. Filled with that remarkable Truth, I felt a peace surpassing words wash over me.

"All systems go!" I heard myself say, which swept me off into the magnificence of the day when Gail and I would meet again. The day when we were one step closer to fulfilling our mutual goal: deliver Humanity's Truths and a way to awaken for their achievement of peace on Earth.

Chapter 8

Truth

In early July, on the day Gail was returning, I anxiously awaited her arrival. Anxiously, meaning eagerly, because her return signified my calling was progressing! Our reunion's timing was impeccable because my home, life, and emotional wellbeing were now in good order. Thankfully, I had finally reached the place where my state of mind could support a collaborative effort.

On her approach, I welcomed Gail with a wide-open heart. She received me in the same fashion and then affectionately wrapped her *of the Light* essence around me. Grateful for the opportunity to serve with this remarkable humanitarian, I quietly thanked her highest self in consciousness for leading her to me.

Fidgeting about and not wasting a single second, Gail announced, "I'm ready to begin!" Then she informed me exuberantly it was time to launch her "official" line of questioning.

"Can I share my *Q and A* with you?" she asked, while taking a seat.

"Hmm…" I considered. "Let's hold off on that, because there are some details to discuss for clarity's sake."

"Oh…" Her smile faded. "I was looking forward to sharing them. I put a lot of time and thought into their arrangements."

Feeling her disappointment and appreciating her effort, I encouraged her to share them with me. With my suggestion, Gail enthusiastically perched herself on the edge of the sofa.

"My questions are… Is it possible for Humanity to live in peace? Why is Humanity not living in peace? How can an individual and Humanity awaken? How will Humanity achieve peace on Earth? And, finally, how can I help others awaken to facilitate peace?"

"Wow! Well done!" I enthused, impressed with the efficiency of her questions.

She blushed. "Thank you. It took more than two weeks for me to find my way, but it was well worth the effort. So, what do we need to talk about before we can begin?"

"We need to discuss the terms and conditions in how we'll proceed. Specifically, how we are to collaborate and present the *Awakening Plan for Peace.*"

"Then let's get to it!" Gail motioned with her hands.

"Let's!" I tossed a smile her way.

"Okay," I began, "there are two topics to cover, *Truth* and *Beliefs*. We'll start with Truth because Humanity has decided they'll now awaken with Truth. Therefore, that's the platform we'll assist them from."

"Not true," Gail firmly stated, shaking her head repeatedly. "Humanity already chose to awaken with love. After all, love is the healer of all that ails them. It's also their guaranteed means and way to peace."

"Really?" I softly chuckled, since her reaction had proven the need for transparency before we advanced.

"Yes," she nodded.

"Then why hasn't waking with love and solutions presented in its name resolved Humanity's most dire issues?" I asked. "Like wars, racism, violence, and poverty?"

"I don't know," Gail shrugged.

"It's because love on Earth can no longer resolve those issues."

"But it can." She tensed. "We just need to keep at it. Focus our efforts on expressing our love for one another and show kind demonstrations of it. Then, everyone will awaken, and peace will prevail."

"Hmm…" I swung my head side to side. "Sadly, that's not true, despite many on Earth believing it is."

"What do you mean?" she asked, looking confused and determined. "Love is and always will be Humanity's saving grace."

"I hear you, Gail, as love is an important component in how to live harmoniously. The problem is, Humanity's version of love is riddled with expectations. Expectations that feed and support fear and division, not peace. Therefore," I stated again, "it was decided Humanity will awaken with Truth."

"Who decided that?" Her eyes narrowed.

"The Mortal Majority," I reminded her.

"Then why do the most highly awakened spiritual teachers say that love is the way to peace?"

"They say it because *unconditional love* is a way to peace. Additionally, it's what can end fear's rule. Unfortunately, despite many enlightened teachers explaining the benefits of abiding by love, that's not the kind of love used and practiced on Earth."

"Oh…" Gail dropped her shoulders. "Did the veil have something to do with this?"

"It did, and that's why Humanity has searched for what love is ever since. It's also why people on Earth feel like love always falls short of what their hearts want most.

"Therefore," I emphasized, yet again, "Humanity's Awakening will happen with Truth."

"Hmm…" Gail turned her eyes skyward, looking as though she were casting a butterfly net with them. "I guess I did ask for *Truth, Clarity, and Hope* to help Humanity awaken, not love. So, I must have already known what was needed, even though Humanity believes love is the way to peace."

"Yes, you did." I smiled with her remembrance. Then, since she was clear on that topic, I asked, "Are you ready for the next Truth disclosure?"

"I am."

"Perfect. The next item is," I locked eyes with her due to its importance, "the Truths you've come to receive, the ones within the *Awakening Plan*, will by default commence your Awakening. I share this because if you are not ready for that outcome, we need to wait before moving forward."

Gail considered what I had said, her expression thoughtful. "I'm more than ready to awaken. Yet, with the way you've phrased this, I'm guessing there's more to your point."

"There is," I confirmed. "My point is, when you commence your ascent in consciousness, everything that needs addressing will automatically rise to the surface to show what needs correcting."

Gail laughed. "Like the defensive reaction I just had about Humanity waking with Truth?"

"Yes, like that." I laughed too.

"What needs correcting in this situation, with how I reacted?"

"First, it's your resolve that everything taught on Earth is Truth. Which," I offered, "has you immediately distrusting anything that's not of Humanity's beliefs. Then, it's your resistive predisposition, which is driven by your human nature."

"My 'resistive predisposition, driven by my human nature?' " She squinted. "What's that even mean?"

"It means that your natural tendency is to resist less gratifying solutions. For instance, you adamantly defended love as the fix-all for Humanity's issues, rather than Truth."

"Oh… I think I get it," she paused, while processing my suggestion. "My human nature is to pursue *pleasurable resolutions*. Therefore, I insisted that love was the answer to Humanity's problems. That's because love is *a feel-good solution*."

"Yes!" I said excitedly, for her ease of clarity.

"Wow… I guess I'll need to work through my 'resistive predisposition,' like only wanting to embrace solutions that I favor and find more appealing. Especially," she emphasized, "if it's affecting something of importance, like achieving peace and my Awakening. Also," she added, "I'll need to practice discernment in what I believe is Truth."

"That's an excellent approach, Gail."

"Thanks. And with my new understanding, I want to apologize for my defensiveness. I guess Truth causes unexpected reactions even for me."

"No worries, your reactions will better equip you to help others who are experiencing the same. And I'll give you a tip," I offered, to bring the point I was making full-circle, "when you want to identify what needs improving, look to the strong reactions you are having. Because you can use those to identify your hurdles, the ones that hinder your progress."

"That's a great suggestion." Gail then said to herself, so as not to forget, "When feeling defensive and protective toward what I believe, I'll find what's of issue and needs addressing."

"Exactly. And know," I assured her, "your reaction was mild. You shifted quickly into accepting the Truths shared. For others, though, tolerating Truths not of Humanity's core beliefs can be difficult."

"I see that. Though," she added, "their issues are not only with Truth because people on Earth are equally reactive and overly argumentative toward any belief not aligned with their own. We know it's due to fear, even though it shows up as anger, defensiveness, and distrust."

"Pure Truth. Note, though, that your reaction wasn't due to a fear you have. Instead, it was just a reactive habit exposing itself for transformation."

"Understood," she said, then she drifted off to another place.

"Where are you?" I asked.

"Oh," she looked back toward me, "I'm wondering if we can address my questions now."

"Not yet. There's more to cover. For instance, when I teach Truth, it can feel cold and uncaring. Know, though, that's not my intention because I care deeply about your and Humanity's wellbeing during your conscious ascension."

Gail tilted her head, looking unclear.

"The reason Truth and even I can feel uncaring," I explained, "is because we are factual and waste no time getting straight to the point. Equally, we present this way because we don't take to coddling or pacifying since those would defeat our singular purpose. Which is, to help Humanity consciously ascend with Truth's transformative abilities."

"Oh, I get it. You and Truth don't emotionally engage. Otherwise, this way to awaken would lose its effectiveness."

"Exactly, as my job is to stand in the place of Truth for another until they can reach that place for themselves. I carry no one because if I did, they'd not awaken and would remain stuck in situations that need overcoming. For instance, victimization, fear, and 'the not so good enoughs.' "

"That I understand because I work with people in the same way. I carry no one, I don't coddle, and I definitely do not support codependent commiseration."

I shook my head and smiled with my eyes. "Yes! No commiserating! Because commiseration is a trap everyone must avoid falling into if waking is their goal."

I paused momentarily and then asked, "Are we clear to this point?"

"Yes."

"Perfect. The next disclosure is the most important to me because I need to ensure the ultimate Truth is understood. Otherwise, the *Awakening Plan for Peace* could appear to contradict what Truth is.

"Here goes…" I said, "the Truth of the Truth is that there's absolutely no need for an *Awakening Plan for Peace*, nor using its instruction to awaken. That's because one's Awakening can be achieved by using the principles of Truth only. Simply practice them daily and bathe yourself in their stream of consciousness… and then you will automatically align with Truth and its all-knowingness. The result is that you will consciously ascend, and peace will prevail as your primary experience."

"That's breathtaking…" Gail inhaled the essence of Truth. "I can actually feel its abilities. With how amazing this feels, why are we not helping Humanity awaken with Truth's principles and consciousness?"

"It's because it was already tried, multiple times, by numerous phenomenal teachers. Unfortunately, their efforts did not have the desired outcome, which was to get the whole of Humanity to peace."

"Why not?"

"Mostly, because waking in Truth requires one detaching their mortal mind from needing to understand how Truth works. Also, because the fundamental principles taught in how to awaken this way massively contradict what Humanity believes."

"And the Truth principles are?"

"There are many, but the ones that challenge Humanity's beliefs the most are that good and bad and wrong and right doesn't exist. Neither do disease, poverty, evil, harm, malice, and death."

"Holy cow!" Gail blurted, surprised with the concept. "I can see the challenge in people accepting all that as Truth."

"Right? And accepting those are key to accomplishing an Awakening with *the principles of Truth*. Fortunately, for Humanity, *the Truths of whom they are* will prove far less challenging.

"You know, Gail, if Humanity simply quit telling stories about themselves and each other, their issues on Earth would resolve rather quickly. The stories that caused them to divide and turn on one another. The stories that still today endlessly perpetuate violence, racism, and hate."

"Imagine that. It's so simple…" She easily connected with the premise. "All they must do is quit telling stories causing harm, then one day Humanity will reach peace."

"That's correct. "

"Brilliant!" she cheered. "Let's help Humanity awaken with that suggestion!"

"We will!" I assured her. "Because *not telling stories* that cause harm is a part of the solution you've come to receive. It's one of the principles that established the *Awakening Plan for Peace*. In total, they are *Start Being the Change Today, Choose Your Stories Wisely, Love More than You Fear, Create Consciously and Responsibly,* and *Seek the Best and Highest for All.*"

"I love these!" Gail threw a "Yay!" my way. "Let's use those in total to advance Humanity's Awakening."

I laughed, assuring her we would, and then I moved us forward.

"All right, let's complete our Truth discussion. Summed, regarding waking with the principles of Truth, the Truth is, many on Earth are unable to grasp and awaken with them. First, because they're filled with endless contradictions. Also, because their concepts are far too foreign. And finally, because they require one to abandon what they believe is real and true."

"I imagine so…" Gail nodded, "by saying 'good, bad, wrong, right, disease, poverty, and death don't exist.' "

"Exactly, because those Truths challenge mortal minds greater than anything else. Therefore, after centuries of failed attempts to help Humanity awaken this way, it was decided things need to change up.

"Hence, the *Awakening Plan for Peace*. A plan that will help Humanity awaken with an account of their historic Truths, versus them having to do so with Truth's elusive principles. A means and way created and calibrated to help Humanity consciously ascend to achieve peace. Specifically designed," I highlighted, "to be used within *The Illusion*, the place where Truth's tenets and Humanity's beliefs most frequently clash."

"Fantastic! That's exactly what I've come to receive!" Gail clapped her hands.

"Fabulous!" I clapped my hands with her, also for my next announcement. "And, Gail, I'm happy to report, we can now proceed with the topic of *Beliefs*. Do you have any questions before we advance?"

"No, not currently. But if it's okay, I'd like to sum the two ways one can awaken with Truth. I want to make sure I'm clear so I can explain it to others."

"Sure, give it a go."

"The first way one can awaken *with Truth* is through utilizing its principles. Also, by immersing oneself into its stream of consciousness. Both of which are spiritual paths and practices.

"Another way to awaken *with Truth* is with the *Awakening Plan for Peace*, a plan founded on Humanity's Truths. The *Awakening Plan* is available for those who have difficulties with abstracts and hypotheticals. And," she added, "though this way to peace may seem to contradict Truth, it still has the ability to achieve peace."

"Yes!" I threw my arms into the air. Then, I noted to myself how well she was doing, and thought, "Let's see how well she fares with *Beliefs* since that topic is one of the most highly debated on Planet Earth."

Chapter 9

Beliefs

"On to *Beliefs* we go…" I announced, after a 5-minute review of my notes.

"One step closer to *Q and A*…" Gail softly clapped.

"That's correct," I nodded, and then I dropped us into our discussion.

"As said, Gail, the topic is now *Beliefs*, specifically yours, mine, and Humanity's. And the first recommendation is that we leave our beliefs out of the equation in how Humanity awakens. Of course, Humanity has a choice in the matter. Yet," I locked eyes with her, "you and I do not, since we are required to not speak of our personal beliefs while presenting the *Awakening Plan*."

"Really?" she asked.

"Yes. It's a mandated requirement per the terms of my calling, which I disclosed to you when we first met. Therefore, because you are now my collaborative partner, those terms are equally applicable to you."

"I know, but are you speaking about spiritual beliefs? Because that's not easy to do," she said, reaching for her heart. "It's a sad request if you ask me."

"I am speaking of spiritual beliefs," I confirmed.

"And realize, Gail, this condition was difficult for me to accept also, as not speaking of my love and dedication for whom I serve beyond seemed nearly impossible. Even so, I understand the need for this approach because personal beliefs and how they're used on Earth are precisely what keeps Humanity from peace."

"Okay…" Gail thought about it. "If beliefs are to stay out of the equation, does that mean faith's out also? Because if so, that's a sad prospect too."

"No, faith is still in," I assured her. "Because many can effectively awaken with faith-based practices. Though that's true, many on Earth currently resist faith as a way to peace. Hence, another reason there's a need for an *Awakening Plan*."

"Why is faith resisted as a solution?"

"There are many reasons that I will detail later. In short, though, it's because the Truths delivered to facilitate peace were misused. They were taken, manipulated, and even hidden so that only a handful of humans could fulfill their private agendas. Individuals also used Truth to maintain their rule over the masses. This ultimately resulted in people not knowing what Truths to believe or have faith in."

"Makes sense, yet with knowing this," Gail's brow scrunched, "now my concern is, what if Humanity thinks you're trying to manipulate them with Truth too?"

"Great question. People will know I'm not manipulating them because I don't insist they do anything with their Truths. I'm only delivering them and helping with their assimilation, if requested. Additionally, I'm not asking anyone to practice faith, or believe in what I'm presenting."

"But how will Humanity know the Truths you're sharing are really theirs?"

"They'll know because the Truths I share will stir their immortal knowings. Then, they'll activate an eternal memory bank within each of them. Which, ultimately, will have these Truths resonating deeply within those who encounter them.

"And, I have a question for you, Gail," I continued, knowing it would further her understanding. "Thus far, why have you so easily accepted the Truths I've disclosed are actually Truth?"

"Um…" she considered before answering, "it's because when I read your chapter in *Pebbles in the Pond*, I instinctively knew everything you shared was real and true. I never questioned it."

"Exactly. You easily recognized Truth. That's how it'll work for others too. Therefore, for those who cannot awaken with faith, they can do so instead with the resonation of Truth. That means the greatest gift we'll give Humanity is their Truths."

"Got it," she confirmed.

"Okay, back to *Beliefs*," I pressed forward. "We've established you and I cannot intermix our personal beliefs with the Truths we deliver. What I want to highlight next is that if Humanity follows our lead and leaves their beliefs out of the equation too, they'll have an excellent chance of restoring peace. That's because it's their beliefs and resulting biases that give rise to their most difficult issues."

"So…" she deliberated, "if Humanity takes their beliefs out of the mix, and is mindful about the stories they tell, then they'll achieve peace? Their destruction of one another will no longer take place?"

"Yes," I answered. "Yet, to achieve peace entirely, they must also quit judging one another and resolve the biases they've accumulated. Then, the entire planet and all living on it can transition into an era of reconciliation. It's so simple, right?"

"I guess…" she shrugged.

I shook my head no, indicating it was just an inference.

"I only wish that were true," I stated. "Unfortunately, it's not, since humans will fight to the bitter end to defend what they believe. Resulting in them going to battle to destroy one another over their theories on who is right, wrong, good, bad, and evil. Their beliefs then lead them to judge, condemn, hate, maim, and kill those who don't believe as they do."

Gail gasped and then cradled her head with her hands.

I bit my lip deeply, disturbed by my choice of words.

"Gail, I'm so sorry I dropped that on you so quickly. Sometimes I forget it's not just about disclosing the facts, while needing to keep myself emotionally detached from it all. If I don't, with all I feel, I would not accomplish my calling."

Gail slowly looked up, her eyes filled with sorrow. "Why do they keep treating each other so horribly? Why do they continue fearing and destroying one other when all it takes is giving up their beliefs to get to peace?"

"Well…" I exhaled deeply, also saddened by all that was happening, "that's a very long story. This we will discuss when we cover how Humanity descended in consciousness."

"But can you just share the underlying issue? What's happening to cause all of this?"

"Sure. This is happening because Humanity feels *unsafe*. And because they do, they repeatedly promote the premise that *the world they live in is a dangerous place.*"

"Unsafe? That's why they do the things they do?"

"Yes."

"Why do they feel unsafe?"

"Mostly, it's because of the stories they tell. Though true, it's also because they veiled and cut themselves off from their primary support systems… *the Light*, Truth, unconditional love, and that which gifted them this incredible experience."

"Oh…" Gail reached for her heart. "I understand feeling unsafe now. And though you're not telling me the *whole story* yet, I'm beginning to understand there are many reasons why beliefs cannot be a part of Humanity's Awakening."

"Yes, there are many. And if people don't curb their beliefs and give others the space they need to awaken, then Humanity collectively will never reach peace. Bottom line, everyone must quit insisting others believe as they do, and then each beautiful human being can successfully navigate their rise in consciousness."

We sat quietly for several moments, after which Gail said, "Please tell me the *Awakening Plan for Peace* can resolve their issues, so they quit hurting and destroying one another."

"It can, Gail, I promise."

Not wanting to further her sadness, and since I had covered the *Beliefs* topic sufficiently, I decided to end our discussion. Out of courtesy, I asked if she had any other questions.

"No questions," she replied. "Just a comment. Now that I know how this all works, I promise not to disclose or speak to my personal beliefs."

"Thank you. And guess what?" I smiled, hoping my next words would lift her spirits. "Disclosures are complete, that means we can now begin *Q and A!*"

Gail only half-smiled, which I understood with how careless I was with my previous words.

After taking a moment to assess the situation, I asked, "Would you like a few days to process what we've discussed? Then we can officially launch your *Q and A* on a happier note? Because…" I lingered, excited for what was ahead, "the Truths I'll share next are the most fascinating of all."

"Yes, please, that would be best," she replied. "Because a fresh start with a happier heart is how I'd like to begin. How about next week? Then I can prepare my emotional self to receive higher doses of Truth."

"That works," I replied, and then I went and sat next to her and took her hands into mine.

"Gail, I am sorry I hurt your heart. And know, though moments like these will surface along the way, there's nothing we can't overcome if we stand unified in Truth. We have shared abilities as Truth-Seekers, and we're perfectly matched to manage the difficulties."

"I'll be okay..." Gail whispered, her eyes glistening. "I just need to remember the Truths I have come to receive are not going to be all dressed up in nice and pretty." She then scooted closer to me while connecting her heart with mine. "Thank you for collaborating with me and delivering the Truths we need on Earth."

"You're welcome. And thank you for receiving what I'm here to deliver."

Mutually knowing it was time to part ways, we stood, came together, and lovingly embraced one another in reverence for how we each served. After resting in the comfort of our growing bond, Gail connected her heart to mine one last time and gazed into my eyes while saying, "I see you and I am grateful for all you do."

I placed my hand over my heart and repeated the same with rising emotion, "I see you and I am grateful for all you do."

I then looked beyond this realm, to all who have contributed to getting my calling back on track, and whispered, "Grateful beyond measure..."

"Until soon..." Gail turned and then left.

After parting ways, though the initiation of our collaborative quest had not played out as planned, I was neither worried nor concerned.

Instead, I was grateful to confirm we could effectively navigate the hurdles we would encounter. Sure, moments like these would arise; yet as we proved today, we were up for the challenge and would find our way.

Chapter 10

The Commencement of Q and A

"It's *Q and A* day!"

"What!" I startled out of a deep sleep, covered in goosebumps with Gail's proclamation.

"What time does she wake up?" I looked at my cellphone, and I saw it was 5:15 a.m.

"Really?" I thought, then I laughed since sudden wake-up calls are quite common for me. In the early morning hours, Those beyond frequently rouse me from a slumber. I scurry out of bed, retrieve pen and paper, and quickly list all items for that day's agenda. Even so, it was rare for anyone to awaken me in the way Gail just had. Of course, it was not an issue because I, too, was thrilled it was *Q and A* day!

Though it was an early wake-up call for a night-owl like me, I decided to start my day.

While puttering about and completing my chores, I noticed an overwhelming surge of enthusiasm increasing within. I soon realized this was due to Gail's and my excitement. It was also due to rising anticipation taking place beyond the veil. How could it not, with Humanity's souls as the Mortal Majority celebrating the possibility of the *Awakening Plan's* delivery.

Realizing I would need to practice mindfulness in how I allowed their eagerness to affect me, I decided to take control of the situation. Without careful management, their over-the-top excitement could keep me from presenting all I was to convey. To avoid this outcome, I took a seat on the floor and purposefully tempered their celebratory effects. This, fortunately, helped me release what was not of benefit.

When I achieved better equilibrium, I tuned in to hear the suggestions for today's agenda. Specifically, how Gail and I were to proceed, and to my surprise and delight, the recommendation was we travel to the realm of Truth to start our *Q and A*! I hoped she approved, because it was the perfect place to share Humanity's initial Truths with fear unable to interfere there. Either way, here or beyond, I continued preparing for Gail's arrival, knowing all would align for an ideal outcome.

Three hours after Gail's first announcement, she approached and exclaimed, "It's *Q and A* day!"

"I know! I heard you earlier this morning," I laughed.

Gail laughed too, as she brushed past me without a hello. Then, after taking a seat on the sofa, she said, "I can't believe this day has finally come with you delivering and me receiving Humanity's highest Truths. I'm so excited. Let's begin!"

"I'm excited too," I said, while seating myself in the chair across the room. "But there's something we need to discuss first."

"No..." Gail playfully moaned. "More disclosures?"

"Nope, disclosures are complete."

"Then what?"

"I was wondering..." I lingered, hoping she would say yes, "if you'd be willing to have our *Q and A* take place in another location?"

"Take time to go elsewhere?" Gail looked about the room.

"Yes."

"Mmm, I'm not sure. How much time will it take to relocate?"

"We'll lose little time in doing so," I assured her, knowing she would want to begin immediately.

"Well..." she considered. "Where are you suggesting we go?"

"To the dimensional realm of Truth." I held my breath, unsure how she would react.

"Where?"

"The dimensional realm of Truth," I repeated. "The place where I have lived and worked since the beginning of my existence."

"I'm confused," she squinted. "And I have absolutely no idea what you're talking about."

"I imagine…" I trailed off, realizing she most likely had never heard of my home since it's located in the furthest reaches of the multi-realm Universe. Knowing she would need assistance with understanding, I sat on the floor and positioned myself before her. I then took a moment to assess how to best explain the opportunity before us. When I found a solution, I leaned in to help her find her way.

"Gail, you came to me to receive the Truths I found, correct?"

"Yes."

"And you want to know the entire account of Humanity's existence, the *whole story*, right?"

"I do."

"Then know the dimensional realm of Truth is the best location for you to receive Humanity's highest Truths. With that understanding, how about we visit the place where you can receive Truth, minus the constraints of the veil and fear?"

"I guess my answer's yes…" she replied, as she drifted in thought while chewing her lip.

Knowing her conscious agreement was mandatory, I paused, considering how to further her along. When I saw how to do so, I scooted closer to her.

"Gail," I said, while lightly touching her knee to refocus her attention, "I want you to do something for me. Take a moment to quiet yourself, then connect with *you* as your highest self in consciousness. When you're centered, ask the following question. 'Does this person have the highest Truths I seek to help Humanity?' After receiving the answer, ask, 'Is going to the realm of Truth of benefit or detriment to me?' When complete, let me know, and we'll discuss what you received."

"Okay," she agreed.

To allow her space, I went outside and took a seat on the front porch to enjoy the summer weather. I then closed my eyes to rest in preparation for our time ahead. It was not until I heard the door open that I realized I had fallen asleep.

"Ready?" I stood, looking to Gail.

"I am," she replied, while stepping back into the house.

I followed and took a seat on the sofa next to her.

"What answers did you receive?"

"Well..." she said, "I'll do my best to explain it all. Know, though, that I'm unsure I'll do so in an understandable way, so please have patience with me."

"Take your time," I told her. "And know that however you share your experience is exactly how it's to unfold." I then quieted myself until she found her way.

Gail took in a deep breath, let it out with a giant exhale, and then began.

"When I connected with my highest self, I posed the first question you told me to ask, which was about whether you have the highest Truths I seek. I was immediately told 'Yes' you do. I was also told I don't have to question if you're sharing Truth or not because Truth is all you can speak. I then received confirmation that you have all components needed to help Humanity awaken and return to peace. And since my calling is getting them to that destination, my heart filled with the assurance I needed. Sure, I thought it was all possible," Gail looked to me, "yet I guess I needed clarity.

"After that," she continued, without pausing, "I received confirmation the *Awakening Plan for Peace* can help resolve the conflicts on Earth. I'm sure that was mentioned because when we last met, my heart was worrying about whether the terrible things happening on Earth would ever end. I was also told that the *Awakening Plan* would help Humanity clearly understand how they ended up living in an unawakened state of consciousness. Understanding this will help them accept responsibility for all the issues they created."

Gail paused, so I took the opportunity to enjoy the insights she had received. After a moment, she continued.

"This next part, I found interesting, and I thought it was important to know. I was told your job is to provide the details needed for Humanity to awaken. Yet, in the end, it's for myself and those who serve like me to teach and assist the masses because we can do so with greater ease. Meaning," she laughed, "we'll have to help translate because the way you share Truth makes it difficult for people to understand."

I rolled my eyes and laughed because her last statement was beyond accurate.

"In closing to this topic," Gail continued, "it was made quite clear that I, those who serve like me, and all highly-awakened people on Earth are key to the *Awakening Plan's* success. Humanity's Awakening and return to peace is for *us* to achieve. It's not for you and those who serve in the realm of Truth to expedite, since you are only a designated resource for the Truths we need."

I nodded that it was true, with tears oncoming. First, because the last message shared was imperative for her to know. The message was: the achievement of peace on Earth is dependent on those who serve like her and Humanity's efforts solely. Second, because I could see the incredible arrangements taking place here and *There* to help Gail with her decision.

"Would you like to know what was said about going to the realm of Truth?" Gail interrupted my thoughts.

"Of course," I replied, smiling.

"Well, that discussion didn't go as expected because my higher self wasn't the one who answered. Instead, my question was addressed from elsewhere."

"Really?" I asked, surprised.

"Yes." She grinned ear to ear.

"And…" I gestured, wanting to know.

"I received a booming 'Yes!' from what sounded like thousands and thousands of people," she enthused. "I was confused at first, and then I realized it was the Mortal Majority who had answered. They told me going to the realm of Truth was a 'brilliant idea' because it would give me a vantage point and clear view of Truth better than anywhere in all of existence. They also told me visiting your realm is a high honor few are granted. They said I'm only the fifth you've taken, yet the reason I'm going is significant since my purpose is greater than most.

"Also," she continued, "they said you and those you serve with are quite exceptional because you have no agenda regarding Humanity's Awakening. Therefore, I will receive all I am seeking, minus personal bias. They also assured me you each would see to my wellbeing while I am away. So, overall," Gail relaxed into the sofa, "it was highly recommended I take this journey with you."

"I couldn't have explained it better myself," I beamed, thrilled with the outcome.

"And," I added, "thank you for your willingness to gain clarity this way. I would never want you thinking I was leading you into a self-serving agenda. After all, I don't have an agenda, other than assisting Humanity with their Awakening and return to peace."

"I know, and I appreciate receiving answers this way because I feel like a participant rather than an observer."

"So happy to hear…" I returned her smile. "That being said," I crossed my fingers, hoping she would agree, "are you ready to go to the realm of Truth and begin *Q and A*?"

"Yes," Gail confidently answered.

"Then let's begin our journey into the beyond…" I excitedly swept my arms upward, high above my head.

I then took a seat in the middle of the room and tapped the floor beside me, indicating that Gail was to join me. When seated, she perfectly positioned herself to face me. This allowed me to place my hands on her knees for connection.

Linked and synchronized in our intention, and with a "We are ready to receive…" stated from beyond, I gazed into her eyes and asked, "Are you ready?"

"Yes…" she whispered.

"Okay, close your eyes and imagine you and I are standing side-by-side. Then reach out and place your hand into mine." I could see she understood because when I closed my own eyes, I saw the image of us standing together with her right hand placed into my left.

As she held onto my hand for dear life, I giggled and again asked, "Ready?"

She closed her eyes tightly and whispered one final time, "Yes…"

With her agreement, I set an intention that I clung to as tightly as she held onto my hand… that on the other side of our journey, Gail would have the ability to receive what I was here to deliver.

Chapter 11

The Dimensional Realm of Truth

"Where are we?" Gail slid her hand from mine.

"We're in the dimensional realm of Truth," I chimed, happy to be home again.

"Hmm…" she hummed, while stepping away to explore where we had landed.

Taking note of her lack of clarity about where we were, I stuck close by to monitor her adjustments. I was not overly concerned, yet I wanted to keep a close eye on her. While doing so, what I found most interesting was that she was gazing upward only—her mouth dangling open. Curious, I began thoroughly evaluating the room in greater detail myself. Of course, this time with the fresh eyes of her new perspective.

The room had an oversized table in its center, measuring over 30 feet long and more than ten feet wide. This was what I thought would have captured Gail's attention first. However, when I tracked her visual path, I immediately saw the room was exceptionally tall compared to its length and width. I understood this arrangement was purposeful, accommodating for the size of Those using it. Yet, with Gail not privy to this information, its height must have seemed beyond significant. How interesting I had not noticed these things before, considering the countless meetings I had attended at this table.

Next, I walked up to the table and approached the seat where I always sat. This caused me to laugh since that seat was the only seat where I was ever allowed to sit. That's because seating arrangements in the realm of Truth were always meticulously assigned. This need for order not only applied to where one sat; it was equally applicable to the number of chairs placed around that table. The number in total was always eight—never more, never less—with three chairs on each side and one at each end. My chair was a center chair, nestled between two others. If I brought guests, they sat on either side of me, and Those we met with occupied the seats across from us. If there were not enough chairs for everyone attending, the remainder of the group would have to stand because no additional chairs were ever added.

Wanting to know how Gail was progressing, I turned my attention back to her. I then asked if she had any questions while seating myself in my usual chair.

Still looking skyward, she asked again, "Where are we?"

"We're in the dimensional realm of Truth," I answered again, while watching her consciousness trying to expand.

"What's that mean?" She shifted her attention, glancing toward me. "As other than the soaring height of the ceiling, it looks like a boardroom where stuffy old men hold private meetings. Though…" she considered, "it also resembles a chamber where Kings and Queens would meet with their courts. After all, the furniture and décor are obviously 1,000 years old… or maybe even older."

I laughed, agreeing, and then elaborated. "This is the place where I meet with Those who assist with my calling on Earth. They are the ones who I have served with since the beginning of my existence."

"Okay…" Gail nodded, then took to wandering again. "What are their names? Those who live here?"

"I don't know," I shrugged.

"What do you mean you don't know?" Gail spun in my direction.

"Simply that…" I shrugged again. "I don't know because the concept of names is irrelevant to how we serve."

Gail looked confused with the notion, so I explained the premise.

"Here's how the naming thing works. The closer one lives to the highest degrees of consciousness, the less need there is for names to identify one another."

Gail paused in thought, trying to track the concept, then gave up within seconds. "Well, you have to call them something when speaking of them. So, what do you call them if you don't know their names?"

"Well, you could ask just about anyone who knows me, and they'd immediately answer your question." I teased by prolonging my answer.

"Come on." She rolled her eyes, looking annoyed. "What do you call them?"

"I call Them…" I finally answered, "*Them* or *They*."

"That's it?"

"Yes. I used to refer to Them as the Committee. Eventually, though, I met another committee in Humanity's realm. So now I usually refer to Them, as *Them or They* only."

"Okay…" Gail thought about it. "Then how do you distinguish Them from everyone else you call they or them?"

"With capital 'T's, of course." I smiled, amused by my solution.

"Really?" She rolled her eyes yet again. "But capital T's don't convey in conversation."

"Trust me, Gail, people know what I'm referring to. Remember, I'm on Earth serving a very specific calling, and it's all I'm ever pursuing. Therefore, it's not difficult for most to follow. If they look confused, I point a finger upward. Note," I added with a grin, "the *they* I just used has a lower case 't'. "

"Whatever…" She half-smiled while approaching the table. "Can I join you?"

"Absolutely." I stood and pulled a chair out for her to sit—one chair to the left from where I was sitting.

Then, instead of taking a seat to her right from where I just stood, I took the seat to her left at the end of the table, since it is where I was told to sit when we arrived. I know, seating arrangements may seem silly. Yet, sitting where asked would maintain the equilibrium this realm needed. After settling in, I asked Gail how she was feeling.

"I'm good, thank you. I was a little foggy at first, but better now."

"Glad to hear. You know, Gail, you may not realize it yet, but we're perfectly partnered. I know it's true with how easily you're acclimating to this realm."

Gail raised an eyebrow and smirked, "I already knew that would happen because I am a seeker of Truth! Besides, it's not like you took me to Mars."

I noted with her clever answer that she was acclimating well.

"So…" Gail squinted, sizing things up again, "tell me more about this room."

"Well, as I said, this is where I come to meet with Those I serve with. Likewise, this is the place I call home when I'm not on assignment like I currently am."

"This is your home? Where you actually live?" Her eyes grew wide.

"Yes, it is," I confirmed, though I had mentioned this before leaving Earth. Yet, I understood her questioning it again, with her adjusting to all she was experiencing.

"Okay…" Gail lingered, processing. "So, this is the room where you work, not where you live. Right?"

"Actually, Gail, I do live in this room. Additionally, this is where I work full-time when I'm serving in this realm. In fact, 99% of the time I spend here is within this room only."

Gail scrunched her face, looking doubtful.

I smiled and gave her a long, slow nod that it was true.

"Also," I continued, "all who exist and serve from this location live and work full-time from this room too."

"If that's true, where is everyone?"

"They left so we could have the place to ourselves."

"Why?" she asked.

"Because you are currently unable to withstand Their massive states-of-consciousness," I answered. "Also, because your consciousness lacks the ability to comprehend the Truths of whom They are."

"Whoa…" Gail shivered, as though she could see Them.

I softly chuckled, with her curiosity now outpacing her previous doubts.

"Is Their 'massive' size why the room is so tall?" She glanced upward. "Why it's nearly ten stories high?"

"Yes, since it needs to accommodate for Their size overall. Not only for Their height but also for Their energetic compositions and capacities. And know, Gail, this room was downsized for your benefit. If it had been left as it was, you might have gotten lost in its infinities…"

Gail shivered again and held her hands up as if telling me to stop. "Let's postpone the details about this realm for another day. I'd like to maintain my learning abilities for the Truths I've come to receive."

I tilted my head, unclear to her point.

"It's just… it's a lot to take in. And those Truths are excessively stirring my immortal knowings," she giggled. "They're making it nearly impossible for me to process anything."

"Understood," I said, knowing Truth's effects far too well. "Do you feel centered enough to proceed, or do you need additional time?"

"No, I'm ready. Yet, there's something I want to convey first." Gail stood, stepped far from the table, and tilted her head up to the beyond while performing a full-circle twirl.

"Thank you! And thank you again to all who've made this possible!"

"And thank you," she turned to face me, "for trusting me and giving me this once in an existence opportunity. I thank Those you serve with here, and I thank Those who gifted me my incredible calling."

She then paused, looked about the room with a small head shake, and murmured, "The dimensional realm of Truth. Imagine that…"

"Oh, Gail!" I enthused, while standing and taking her hands into mine. "It's you who deserves these praises more than anyone else. Because without you, the *Awakening Plan for Peace* and Humanity's Truths might not deliver. Thank you for showing up when I needed you most and calling me out of hiding."

With our endearments complete, and our hearts overflowing, we shared one of the most endearing embraces I have ever experienced. Then, with our excitement building to commence our journey, I stepped back to receive her properly. This I did, fashioned to her perception of my home, with a perfectly executed curtsy. I followed that with a full-circle twirl of my own.

"Dear Gail," I then said, "welcome to our fantastic, remarkable world…"

Chapter 12

The Awakening Plan for Peace

After receiving Gail on behalf of us all and with her faring well, I suggested we take our seats. While settling into our assigned chairs, I pulled a white binder sitting on the table toward me. I sensed a rise in Gail's curiosity, which she confirmed when she asked what it was.

With her perfect lead-in, I answered, "It's the *Awakening Plan for Peace.*"

"It's finished?" She gently touched it, as though it were the most coveted treasure she had ever encountered.

Smiling widely, I slowly nodded an exaggerated yes.

"Everything? Everything I've come to retrieve to help Humanity awaken?"

"Yes, it's all here," I touched the binder too, "readied and organized for a veiled human to receive."

"Incredible," Gail looked at me, "you must be pleased. This is quite an achievement."

"It certainly is…" I admitted.

"However," I added, while picking it up and holding it before me, "its abilities and importance are not about me. Instead, they are about the great things the *Awakening Plan* can accomplish. Fortunately for me, I'm the one who was asked to take the magnificent, mind-bending journey to locate all the Truths found within it."

"Why mind-bending? Since you can access the information so easily with being unveiled?" she asked.

Shaking my head while laughing, I placed the white binder back on the table.

"It was mind-bending because I had to convert my findings into words! Imagine trying to take Humanity's Truths, patterns, threads, and history all the way back to where nothing exists, and then translating it so it can be understood. Remember that I'm in a body with an earthly mind, therefore the experience was beyond mind-bending!"

"Okay, I think I understand…" Gail giggled, while scanning the realm of Truth, "because I can't explain everything I'm experiencing right now with words either."

"Right?" I smiled, with her now clearly understanding.

Gail nodded and then turned her focus back to the binder again. "Thank you for completing this. I'm so grateful."

"It was my pleasure. Yet," I noted, wanting to give credit where credit was due, "do you know what the driving force was behind the *Awakening Plan*'s completion?"

Gail shook her head no.

"It was you," I told her. "You stood before me and asked the necessary questions to expedite its formulation. Which, in turn, brought about its completion sooner than expected."

Hoping to refresh her memory, I continued, "Gail, your questions were, What are the Truths of what we cannot see? What are the Truths of Humanity? Who are we? What are we? What else exists?"

"Hmm…" Gail closed her eyes momentarily and then opened them again. "I don't recall visiting or standing before you. Yet, I do remember drifting those questions out into the Universe. It was a very private, endearing moment. The moment when I sent my heart's desire into the highest ethers, hoping one day I'd have a brand-new way to help Humanity reach peace."

"And here we are…" I assured her, "to accomplish that and even more. And Gail," I touched her hand, "thank you for your contribution toward the *Awakening Plan's* completion."

"You're welcome," she replied, nonchalantly.

I chuckled to myself, with her clearly not understanding the significance of her being my muse. Knowing we were both eager to begin, I then leaned toward her and whispered into her ear.

"Guess what, Gail? It's now officially…"

"*Q and A* day!" we cheered together.

"And in consideration of that," I said, "I'd like to explain additional details concerning the *Awakening Plan* and how we'll proceed."

"Okay," Gail agreed, so I began.

"First, the *Awakening Plan* presents Humanity's collective Truths and shows how they came into existence. Additionally, it explains who their ancestors are and who founded and gifted them their exceptional experience. With that, though," I emphasized, "there's so much more the *Awakening Plan* contains.

"For instance, it includes, but is not limited to, an explanation of how all conscious beings and souls came to exist. The Truths of who everyone is… here, *There*, and beyond. How and where others have life experiences outside of Humanity's own. Plus, the conscious encounters we experience contingent on where we live."

"Seriously?" Gail raised her brow.

"Yes, and there's more too…" I winked.

"Like how Humanity was gifted the opportunity to live in autonomy, how they lived in consciousness previously, and key details as to why they collectively descended in consciousness. All of which provides the *Clarity* you requested regarding why they live as they do today, not in peace and unawakened. And, Gail, it also offers the *Hope* you seek, through clear instruction in how all can awaken with the principles the *Awakening Plan* was founded on."

"That's all within…" Gail touched and admired the white binder again.

"And even more still…" I promised.

"Then let's get to it!" She wiggled with anticipation.

"Agreed, and here's how we'll do so.

"First, realize that although you have developed an official *Q and A* list, I will not answer your questions individually. Instead, I'll address your first two questions when I share the account of Humanity's existence. Then, when we're complete, I'll answer your remaining three questions. Make sense?"

"Yes."

"Perfect. That said, Gail, please state your first question aloud, to commence your reception of the *Awakening Plan for Peace.*"

"Absolutely! My first question is... *Is it truly possible for Humanity to live in peace on Earth?*"

"Yes, it is," I answered. "It's more than achievable. And I know it's possible because..." I read from a handout I had pulled from the white binder,

"*...Peace is Humanity's birthright and Divine inheritance, now and evermore.*

"*Living in peace is the only way Humanity ever intended to live.*

"*Peace on Earth is now a Universal goal, supported by All beyond as never before.*

"*Peace on Earth is why you, I, and others are serving as we do.*

"*And peace will come to be... with the Third Intention Humanity set.*"

"I love these! I'm ready to receive!" Gail opened her arms wide.

"Perfect. Then let's begin where all began... with your, my, Humanity's, and every conscious beings' initial inception."

Chapter 13

The Inception and Commencement of You

Knowing what was before us, which still fascinates me to this day, I asked Gail for a moment to myself. With her agreement, I quieted to prepare for what I would share. First, with an expansive breath, to connect with Humanity's Third Intention: *collectively awaken, for the achievement of peace on Earth.* During this process, I asked all souls who were committed to assisting with Humanity's cause to please hold space for the task before me.

Taking yet another deep breath, I next connected with the Truths of every soul's inception since it was the first topic we would discuss. I lingered in that blissful place for quite some time, setting an intention to convey everything in an understandable way. With my final exhale, I centered myself into the incredible journey Gail and I would take to assist with Humanity's Awakening. When I opened my eyes, I found Gail tightly grasping the table.

"Are you okay?" I asked.

"I think so…" she laughed, while steadying herself. "Even though your 'moment to yourself' almost swept me away. Maybe you should've considered tethering me to something before going there? Wherever there was."

"Oh, Gail…" I said, while taking her by the hand.

Feeling more excited than I ever have, I then hurried us to the far end of the room to show her where "there" was! After arriving, I seated her for her best view.

"Ready?" I asked.

She nodded, so I turned and opened two enormous curtains before us. I pulled one to the far right of our view, the other to the left. There was a third curtain hanging horizontally below the two I had just opened, and that one remained closed for the time being.

"Are you serious?" Gail sprang from her seat to join me.

She then paced the twenty-foot span, trying to figure out what I had opened to her. Shortly after, she gently reached forward to touch its vastness, which connected her with the outermost limits of all of existence.

"Wow…" she uttered, "it looks like the entire Universe. So endless… infinite… exquisitely awesome…"

After Gail expressed her endearments and with no forewarning, it suddenly illuminated the room with its *Light-filled* radiance. Surprised it had shown itself to her, and unsure what to do, Gail quickly grasped my hand. We then stood together—awed and amazed—while it warmly wrapped its comfort and peace around us. When it was complete, it leaned itself in and invited us to receive its wisdoms and knowingness.

"Whoa…" we simultaneously gasped, since that was unexpected even for me. And though I was awestruck with the gifts we were given, I held steady, knowing I had to remain intact for Gail's wellbeing.

Gail, though, eyes wide with wonder, murmured, "It's the most beautiful, amazing thing I have ever seen…" Then she physically leaned herself far into it all.

"Hold on there, sister…" I grabbed her and held on tight. After all, she was not prepared or equipped to navigate a return trip from where she was heading.

"Okay…" she took a step back, "but what is that place? It looks like a destination I could actually step into."

"It is. Yet, that destination's not one your consciousness can currently endure. And to answer your question, that is what I call the *All that IS*."

"The *All that IS*?"

"Yes, it's what affords us each the opportunity to come into existence. It's also a location found just beyond the realm of Creation. And know, even though what you're viewing looks like a single destination, there are three positioned within it. The Point of Origin, the Point of Inception, and the dimensional realm of *Light*."

"Oh my…" were her only words.

Knowing it was a lot to take in, I ended my tutorial for the moment. Then I allowed her to explore the *All that IS* up close again, with supervision. This would help her to acclimate to the Truths I would first present. She studied every detail, continued reaching in to experience its significance, and repeatedly expressed "how fantastic!" it all was. When I knew her exposure was reaching its limits, I gently guided her back to her seat.

"Okay, Gail," I said, once she was seated, "welcome to your first glimpse into where the inception, reception, and commencement of all conscious beings takes place. All before you," I turned and gestured toward the *All that IS*, "is what we will initially study. First, so you can understand *how all who exist came into existence*. Then, so you can gain clarity as to *who everyone is in Truth*.

"And, Gail," I held a handout before us after seating myself, "if you're amazed by what's behind curtains number one and number two, you're going to love this!"

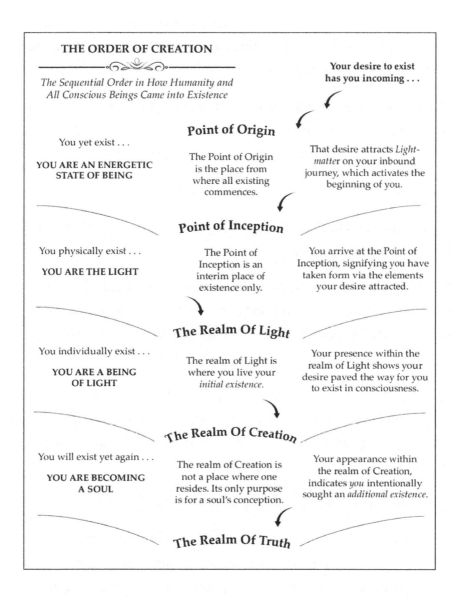

THE ORDER OF CREATION

The Sequential Order in How Humanity and All Conscious Beings Came into Existence

Your desire to exist has you incoming . . .

Point of Origin

You yet exist . . .

YOU ARE AN ENERGETIC STATE OF BEING

The Point of Origin is the place from where all existing commences.

That desire attracts *Light-matter* on your inbound journey, which activates the beginning of you.

Point of Inception

You physically exist . . .

YOU ARE THE LIGHT

The Point of Inception is an interim place of existence only.

You arrive at the Point of Inception, signifying you have taken form via the elements your desire attracted.

The Realm Of Light

You individually exist . . .

YOU ARE A BEING OF LIGHT

The realm of Light is where you live your *initial existence.*

Your presence within the realm of Light shows your desire paved the way for you to exist in consciousness.

The Realm Of Creation

You will exist yet again . . .

YOU ARE BECOMING A SOUL

The realm of Creation is not a place where one resides. Its only purpose is for a soul's conception.

Your appearance within the realm of Creation, indicates *you* intentionally sought an *additional existence.*

The Realm Of Truth

(Dear Reader: visit *www.MyCallingMyQuest.com* to download a more readable illustration in a free PDF format. This includes all handouts within this book.)

"Oh… my… goodness…" Gail looked to me after several minutes had passed. "This is how everything came into existence? It's not just mind-bending, it's mind-blowing!"

"Right?" I excited with her, since for the first time ever, I was allowed to share my most fascinating discoveries. Eager to proceed, I asked, "Are you ready to hear how you came into existence?"

"Absolutely!" She scooted her chair closer to me.

"Great, then let's begin with what's displayed within this illustration." I pointed to the handout.

"Overall, what's shown is all existing within the *All that IS*, from where nothing exists to where you first exist in consciousness. What it also shows, is what I call the *Order of Creation*. I'm unsure how others refer to it, but that's what I named it while I was collecting Humanity's Truths.

"The *Order of Creation*," I explained, "is *the Universal Path* you, I, all souls, and beings take to come into existence. And if you look to the top of the page and carry downward, you'll see the sequential order in how this was achieved. Make sense?"

"Yes," she replied, while studying the handout.

"Perfect, let's start at Point of Origin." I pointed to its location. "This is the place where all who exist incepted and began. I say 'began' because, on this occasion, one only exists in potentiality, not in consciousness or physicality."

"So, I don't exist yet?" Gail looked at me.

"Correct. You, as you exist today, do not. Equally, no one does. Though true, we do exist as a portion of what the *All that IS*, is." I gestured toward what I had opened for her. "As its substance, its essence, and how it existed before its inception. Since it, like we," I turned toward Gail again, "evolved as it exists today… in form, consciousness, and physicality."

"Okay…" Gail paused, processing. "So, the Point of Origin is where my creation takes place?"

"No, it's where your existence initiates."

"I'm confused." She squinted. "I came into existence without being created?"

"Yes."

"Hmm…" she paused in thought, "then who brings me into existence?"

"Technically…" I smiled, excited to share this Truth, "*you* do. The possibility of your existence only happens because of *you*."

"Whoa… how did I accomplish that exceptional task if I don't exist yet?"

"That's an excellent question. You accomplished it through *your desire*. Specifically, a desire you had to exist. You see," I pointed to the handout, "when your desire takes rise, it attracts *Light-matter*, which brings you into existence. Your desire can be likened to a magnet, pulling in all needed for you to take form.

"Once you exist," I continued, "you are then on an inbound course to the Point of Inception… which is poised to receive you so you can commence a physical existence. And it's through *your desire*, Gail, that you now exist as *the Light*."

"*The Light*?" Gail shivered. "I exist as *the Light*?"

"Yes, Gail, you do…" I shivered too, with the richness of this Truth.

I then reached over, touched her heart with the palm of my hand, and said, "Gail, when physical reactions happen like the one you just had, it's how you and others will know when Truth is spoken."

She nodded her head. When I removed my hand, she said, "I know what you say about these reactions is true. I've had many of them when encountering Truth. Goosebumps, shivers, dizziness, and sometimes it feels like a wave washing over me."

I smiled while humming, acknowledging these too were indications.

Gail then went quiet, closed her eyes, possibly to process what I had shared.

While she was away, I drifted off into thought… because for me, how we each incepted was not just a Truth I had found while searching for Humanity's. It was also an actual memory of my own inbound journey that had surfaced in my mid-20's. A memory through recalling it that increased my knowing of Truth exponentially.

Years later, I saw a depiction of how stars are born in a show called *The Universe—The Nebulas* episode. When I watched it, I cried endless, happy tears with seeing the visual likeness of what I had remembered. The moment when I rushed my way from the Point of Origin to the Point of Inception, moving through the highest ethers so I too could exist as *the Light*.

When Gail was complete with her moment, she tapped me on the shoulder and asked, "Are you still here?"

"I am," I smiled, while opening my eyes, "I was just connecting with an experience I once had. Are you ready to continue?"

She nodded and then advanced our discussion.

"So, if I understand correctly, the way I came into existence was," she looked to the illustration, "I departed from the Point of Origin because I had a desire to exist. My desire then had me incoming to the Point of Inception, where *Light-matter* was available for me to physically exist. Resulting in," she gazed at me, "I now exist as *the Light*?"

"Yes, you are *the Light*. The very same *Light*," I emphasized, "the *All that IS* just wrapped us both in."

"*The Light* is who I am…" Gail quietly affirmed to herself.

"That's correct, and it's equally who everyone is, since every conscious being came into existence through the same means and way… *of the Light*. This shows," I importantly noted, "all of Humanity was and still is *the Light*. It also shows, there are absolutely no degrees of separation regarding who Humanity is individually or collectively."

"That means…" Gail looked toward the *All that IS*, "we are *One* as *the Light* itself."

"Truth. And, since everyone is *the Light*," I added to her premise, "we are also its peace and tranquility. This proves reaching peace on Earth is possible, because peace is everyone's legacy, birthright, and who we are from the moment we incept as *the Light*."

"Oh…" Gail thought about it. "Peace is just who everyone is."

"Absolute Truth…" I deeply inhaled, while momentarily closing my eyes.

"You know…" Gail lightly touched my arm to refocus my attention, "your *Order of Creation* illustration will have a huge impact with many on Earth. Especially with those seeking clarity about the origin of who everyone is so they can effectively assist with Humanity's Awakening."

"Yes," I nodded. "We are hoping these Truths will help bridge all degrees of separation Humanity experiences with one another. Additionally, it's hoped these Truths will help Humanity overcome their perceived differences. Because, if they continue insisting there are dissimilarities between themselves and others, they will never awaken or achieve peace."

"Hmm…" Gail looked to the handout again. "It seems much of what Humanity believes is far from the Truth."

"It is."

"Well," Gail confidently stated, "the *Awakening Plan* and Humanity's Truths will resolve that issue."

"Aw…" I pressed my palms together, "thank you for your vote of confidence."

"You're welcome. And," she said, "I'm ready to hear more about my evolving existence."

"Perfect." I held the handout before us again. "Okay, Gail, you've incepted, you were received, and you currently exist as *the Light*. Now that you've reached this place, what happens next is the commencement of your *initial existence*.

"This comes about," I pointed to the illustration, "as you transition from the Point of Inception to the dimensional realm of *Light*. Take note," I emphasized, "your *initial existence* is still of *you* and *your desire* only. And your desire now is to fully exist as *the Light* itself in physicality and in consciousness."

Gail thought about it and then asked, "So the realm of *Light* is where my creation takes place? Since a real-life, conscious existence is what I'll experience next?"

"No…" I slowly shook my head. "Your existence, for now, progresses through *your desire* only."

"Okay." Gail blinked several times. "I brought about my conscious existence? It's really true?"

"Yes, it is. You and your desire are what facilitated it. And through your desire, you'll now exist *in physicality* and in consciousness *as a being of Light*."

"Whoa, I'm a *being* now…" Her eyes sparkled.

"Yes. You're a being with a physicality that's as enormous as Those who live here in the realm of Truth. Also, your consciousness is as grand and expansive as Theirs." I opened my arms wide.

"Seriously?" Her mouth dropped open.

"Yes, seriously," I chuckled. "Additionally, you are a self-directing, self-sufficient, actuality having real-life experiences. A thinking, speaking, individual living amongst a collective of peers."

"Too cool!" Gail enthused. "Do we talk to each other?"

"We do, but it's different than on Earth."

"How so?"

"It's not the same because *beings of Light* only converse with one another in a language composed of harmonic tones."

"Can you talk that way?"

"No." I shook my head, smiling. "However, I can interpret the Truths found within those tones, hence the challenges I faced with Truth's translation."

With no further questions from Gail, I asked, "Are you ready to hear more?"

"Yes, please," she replied.

"We left off where you just facilitated your *initial existence* as a *being of Light*. It's important to know here," I looked at her, "your *initial existence* is equally your *eternal existence*. This indicates your existence as a *being of Light*, in consciousness and physicality, will not terminate if you pursue becoming a soul. Make sense?" I asked, to make sure she understood the significance.

Gail paused thoughtfully, and her eyes smiled, indicating it had.

I motioned for her to share her understanding.

"It means that right now, in this moment, I exist additionally to myself as a human being and myself as a soul. Therefore, technically, there are three of me existing simultaneously. It also means…" she pointed to herself and furthered the concept, "me, as a *being of Light*, *am* my highest consciousness of all."

"Yes!" I thrilled, with the clarity she had displayed.

"What it also means," I moved us forward, "is that you will always and evermore exist as *the Light* itself, no matter the choices you make from this point forward. That said, we've now reached the place where you have some choices to make. Do you remain in the realm of *Light* and exist as a *being of Light* only? Or, do you choose…"

"To be created!" Gail raised her arms into the air. "To become a soul!" She pointed at the handout, indicating she had spied the next step of her evolving existence.

I laughed, as she had yet to realize *this creation of her* was only her first of two.

"Well…" She motioned for my confirmation.

"Yes, Gail," I smiled, "you now have the opportunity to experience the creation of you."

"Yay!" She clapped her hands. "I'm not sure why, but this feels exciting."

"That's because it's a very exciting time for all who make that choice. Understand, though, not every *being of Light* chooses to move forward to have another existence. Therefore, to this point in your experience, you have a choice to make… exist solely as *the Light* in consciousness and physicality, or move on to have a new life experience as a soul."

Gail tilted her head. "Why would a *being of Light* choose to stay versus moving forward?"

"Some make this choice because they desire to see to the wellbeing of all who exist outside *of the Light*," I answered. "After all, there is no greater calling one can serve anywhere within all of existence."

"That makes sense," she nodded. "And my next question is, why would a *being of Light* choose to have a new existence?"

"Because, like you…" I laughed, "they have a fanatical fascination with the act of creation."

"Haha…" Gail playfully smirked. "Really, though, since I made the choice to become a soul, why did I choose that option?"

"You chose that because *you desired* to exist outside of the *All that IS* and because incredible opportunities were awaiting you beyond the realm of Creation.

"Let's say you've decided to have another existence," I continued. "With that choice, you'll now descend into the realm of Creation. After arriving, you and other *beings of Light* gather for what's ahead. Before your new existence advances, though, you have another choice to make. Are you going to have a conventional soul's life experience? Or, are you going to exist to live in service?"

"Who decides if I'm going to serve?"

"Again, it's *you*. The decision is always yours to make. Then, after you've decided, things change in how everything progresses. You see, prior to your creation, your evolving existence was of your making only. Now that you want to exist as a soul? Well, there are other factors involved for that to take place."

"Like what?"

"The question is…" I arched my brow, "*like whom*?"

"Hmm…" She hummed to herself.

I paused, uttering an unintentional "Hmm…" of my own. Then I decided to hold off on that discussion momentarily. I did so because I wanted to make sure she was clear to this point. I then stood and walked toward the *All that IS* with Gail in tow. After arriving, I pointed to all before us, "Does this make sense?"

"Absolutely!" Gail stepped up, pointing to the highest location. "This is the Point of Origin. And I'm curious," she looked at me, "why's it so dark there? It seems so bleak."

"Oh, Gail, it's anything but bleak." I reached up, connecting with its stillness.

"Then what's it like?"

"Well…" I thought about it, "it's the most peaceful place I've ever visited. It may not be filled with *the Light*, but it's also not filled with anything else. When I want to simply *be* and experience the true origin of *me*, this is where I go."

Unable to relate, she continued, "Here's the Point of Inception, below it, you'll find the realm of *Light*, and below that is the realm of Creation."

"Correct," I confirmed her understanding. Then I asked, "Are you ready to hear about your creation?"

"Yes, more than! Yet since we're here, can I please spend a few moments with the *All that IS*?"

"Of course," I answered. Then I stood side-by-side with her to make sure she remained in the realm of Truth. After giving her several moments to herself, I took her hand into mine and softly whispered…

"*Dear Gail, all before you IS You… It's us… It's who we all eternally are. It's what we are capable of, as we are It, and It is we. Equally, Its peace and tranquility are how we intuitively know how to exist. Therefore, peace is possible for all of Humanity… they just need their Truths to achieve it. Then, they will live to their highest potential, as the Light and its peace evermore.*"

When our moment was complete, I led her back to the table where we were initially sitting.

Chapter 14

The Omniscient Divines

Once we had seated ourselves in our assigned chairs at the table, I asked Gail for a few moments to myself. This was so I could prepare for what was on the agenda next. Namely, *how all souls came into existence* and *what else exists beneath the realm of Creation.*

Additionally, on the docket was the introduction of Those whom I love and cherish. Of course, who They were in concept, not in physicality since Their in-person introduction was not on the agenda. That's because Gail's ability to receive Them was still unknown. After completing my review, and eager to resume, I laid the *Order of Creation* handout before us.

"Okay, Gail," I began, "we left off where you and other *beings of Light* have made your way to the realm of Creation. This is the place where you and they will commence your next existence. And as said," I looked at her, "things are changing in how the next version of you progresses.

That is, your opportunity to exist as a soul will not automatically happen just because you desire it."

"Understood," Gail confirmed, while viewing the handout.

"So, what's changed specifically?" I posed the question. "As mentioned, it can be found within the *whom* who is present while you await your creation. Realize, the only things you've encountered along your path to exist so far were *the Light, Light-matter*, and other *beings of Light* who live within the *All that IS*. Now that you're in the realm of Creation, there are new additions to the cast of characters. And They are…" I drum-rolled on the tabletop, excited to bring Them into the mix, "the Omniscient Divines!"

"What?" Gail squinted, tilting her head. "Omniscient Divines?"

"Yes, the Omniscient Divines. They are the ones who assist each *being of Light* with their soul's creation. Equally, They are Those who see to the wellbeing…"

"Gods?" Gail interrupted, tightly knitting her brow. "Meaning plural?"

"Uh…" I paused, confused by her reaction. Then I reminded myself she was veiled and not yet educated in how all came into existence. With that, I calmly responded.

"Gail, I did not say 'Gods,' I said the 'Omniscient Divines.' And," I reminded her, "we're not supposed to bring our personal beliefs into the equation. For instance, naming or debating over who the Divine is or is not."

"I know that." She scowled, looking offended. "But it sounds like you're saying there's more than one God. Are you serious?"

"Wow…" I bit my lip, unsure where we were heading.

"Well?" Gail pressed for an answer.

"Gail, I'm not saying there's more than one God. Instead, I'm saying there's more than one Omniscient as the Divine in embodiment. And…" I added, hoping it would help, "this is a Truth you came to receive, as you asked for the highest of all."

"Maybe so, but this is crazy and unacceptable." She glared at me.

"Well, actually," I raised my brow, "it's no more 'crazy or unacceptable' than what's happening on Earth currently. The place where similar topics cause heated misunderstandings and never-ending debates filled with belief and religious intolerance."

I shook my head with the heartbreak of it all. If this continued, Humanity would never reach peace. Taken with how quickly things had shifted, for a topic near and dear to my heart, I dropped my head into my hands and mumbled, "I need a moment, please…"

Deeply saddened by her misunderstanding, I found myself questioning my ability to guide people on this topic. How could I not? With Gail, a Truth-Seeker, unable to receive or accept this Truth herself. I also questioned disclosing total Truth to Gail, reacting as she was. Unclear how to proceed, I reached out and asked for help.

Shortly after, They came to my rescue, saying, "Remember who you are speaking with today. She is your Truth-Seeking Sister. She can handle these Truths since she trained to help Humanity greater than most. Share them with her, and one day she will know what to do with them. Release your anxiety and work through your fears of causing harm. Equally, your aversion to conflict because the time has come to speak of Us."

I accepted, thanked Them, and tried to open my heart to give her a chance to embrace the Omniscients. I then inhaled deeply, gathering strength, so I would not shut down entirely. When I opened my eyes, I said, "I'm ready."

Not having lost her zest while awaiting my return, Gail repeated, "Gods? The Omniscients are Gods? Meaning more than one?"

"No, Gail," I held steady, "they're not Gods as you're referring to Them."

"Then what are They?" she asked, while throwing some heat my way.

"They are the remarkable beings, who with *your* permission," I very importantly noted, "gifted you the opportunity to have the soul life experience you requested."

"Okay…" Gail sideways glanced at me. "What do you call Them if you don't call them Gods?"

Feeling like her question was a set up for further controversy, I stuck with, "I call Them the Omniscient Divines."

"So, you're holding to there's more than one Creator?" Gail shook her head. "That's so disrespectful."

"Gail, please stop. It's you who's being disrespectful." I finally engaged, feeling protective of Them. I then quieted, not wanting to place my pain for what was happening on Earth onto her.

Though my heart ached deeply for how she reacted, I knew her actions were not a personal attack aimed toward Them. Instead, they were representative of the mass confusion taking place on Earth regarding these matters. God, Gods, Father, Mother, Son, Holy Ghost, the Divine, Source, and the Universe… or maybe nothing exists at all. The list goes on and on, as does the fighting, anger, and destruction.

I then looked to Gail to consider how to proceed and saw that she was shaken by how I had responded.

"I'm sorry. I just don't understand…" she whispered, her expression pained. "Why are you so upset?"

I looked at her, unsure how to articulate an answer with how much emotion these issues drive within me. Nevertheless, she needed to know if we were to continue with our collaborative agreement. Therefore, I did my best to convey it all.

"Gail, I'm sorry too," I apologized for my inadequate communication. "And why am I upset?"

She nodded.

"For several reasons," I took a deep breath. "First, I don't want to do anything to compromise a person's opportunity to awaken. As seen from your reaction regarding the Omniscients, sharing even that could cause issues. The Truth is, I'm terrified of messing this up, turning

Humanity from the Divine even further… because of something I have said or done.

"Look at your aversion to this Truth," I highlighted again, with tears oncoming, "even though you are a Truth-Seeker with abilities to understand Truth greater than most. Bottom line, I don't want all you've come to receive tossed out the door before the *whole story*'s told. Also, before *the Divine Order of Source* is entirely understood."

I then paused to breathe, with this all weighing endlessly on me. After all, I'm here to help, not cause harm. Then I continued, while Gail kindly held space for my need to explain.

"Then there's the issue of my heart breaking over how people on Earth react to what one calls the Divine. It hurts deeply… the press-back, negativity, anger, fear, and judgments. And understand," I looked to her, "my pain is not for the press-back or anger directed toward me and the Truths I deliver. Instead, it's for all that's sent out and projected onto the Divine.

"My goodness…" my voice broke, "on Earth, it seems like no one can talk about what they believe in, or what they have reverence for, without issue. Including judging those who believe in nothing at all. As we know, though, that's on Humanity, since Truth was misused to gain power and dominion over others."

I paused yet again… and then, with my truth shared, I released the river of tears I had held back. Tears for the great love and reverence I have for Those who created our souls' existences, as without Them nothing this side of the *All that IS* would exist at all.

After giving me the time I needed, Gail reached out and gently touched my hand. "I'm sorry I hurt you with how I reacted. And know, I experience sadness over these issues too. It's amazing how reactionary we are by default, and how even I distrust Truth."

Gail paused and then added, "There's a gift in what happened, though. Now I'll know how to help others address their belief issues."

"I know," I agreed, "there's always a gift. The other one is, thankfully, our discussion is taking place here in the realm of Truth out of fear's reach. Otherwise, our progress would have been delayed for days. And, Gail, again, I'm sorry."

"It's my fault for opening Pandora's Box…" she sighed, "by not connecting with this Truth."

Feeling better and more relaxed, I shared, "You know, Gail, the bizarre twist in this all is, despite what many on Earth believe, Humanity's own Omniscient doesn't even care what name it's called currently. Or," I added, "if one even believes in its existence.

"In fact," I continued, "all the Omniscient cares about right now is that each beautiful human being gets the opportunity to know Truth. That's so Humanity can awaken and be freed from pain and suffering no matter how they arrive at that place. Some question this as Truth, yet I assure you it is, as an Omniscient would never abandon Humanity because Truth was compromised for personal gain."

"I know this is Truth," Gail stated. "And, I now clearly understand your sadness and frustration. You love all the Divines, and you care deeply about Humanity's Awakening. Yet, you walk a fine line in how you serve and approach this all."

"A very fine line…" I nodded. "And I never want to hinder the progress Humanity is making."

"I understand," she said. "And I'm certain with who you are and the calling you serve that you will ruin nothing. Since…" she swept her arms before us, "all who originate from within this realm will only be of benefit.

"Speaking of which," she gazed upward, "I have a question for you. When we first arrived, we discussed Those who serve with you. The enormous beings with the massive states of consciousness. Are They by chance the Omniscient Divines?"

"They are!" I thrilled, for her acknowledging my Beloveds.

"So…" she giggled, "do you refer to Them as the Omniscient Divines while serving on Earth?"

"Absolutely not." I side-eyed her, laughing too. "That's to avoid a mishap like the one we just had. Instead, I only call Them, *Them* or *They*."

Gail pondered a moment and then teasingly asked, "Do you have a term of endearment for the Omniscients? Like a personal moniker you favor for how you feel about Them?"

"If I did, I'm not sharing it!" I shook my head adamantly, smiling. "Because there's no way I'm going down that road with you again. Besides," I added, "the agreement is that we not speak of our beliefs, including naming the Divine. Therefore, I'll keep my endearments to myself."

"Fine…" she playfully huffed. "And just so you know, I'm ready to hear how my soul's existence commenced. Also, I'm interested to hear more about the Omniscient Divines."

Ready to move forward myself, I quickly accepted her offer. And realize, though what had happened was not easy, it was also of no issue for me. After all, it's a dance delivering Truth, and how fortunate I was to be dancing with Gail. Sure, toes could get stepped on, slips and falls may occur, yet our perseverance would better equip us to help Humanity with their most challenging issues.

Settling into this understanding, I realized Gail's and my capacity to conquer our difficulties effectively, together, meant landing the *Awakening Plan for Peace* was increasing significantly. Grateful for the clarity and confirmation, I exhaled my relief and prepared to proceed.

Chapter 15

Souls, Realms, and the Making of You

Knowing we had gone off-topic by taking a detour from where we were heading, I decided a brief recap would benefit us both. Before doing so, I took a moment to review the material we were still to discuss: *how all souls who exist came into existence* and *what else exists beneath the realm of Creation.*

When I was complete, I asked Gail if she was ready to continue. With her yes, I closed the white binder and neatly stacked my notes before me. Also, I placed the *Order of Creation* illustration before us both to refer to if needed.

"Okay, Gail, to this point," I began, while turning my chair to face her, "we have discussed the inception, reception, and commencement of you. This came about due to a desire you had to come into existence, first, as *the Light* itself. Then, in form and consciousness, as a *being of Light*.

"We've also established," I continued, "as a *being of Light*, you consciously decided to move forward from the realm of *Light* to have *your first intended by you existence*. The operative words here are, *you consciously decided* to exist in yet another way."

"Got it," she nodded. "I became a *being of Light* through my desire only. That means my *initial existence* was unplanned and unintentional. Now that I want to have a soul's life experience? Well, it's intentional and purposeful."

"Exactly, it's intentional. And not by coincidence," I noted, "that's why it's called your *first intentional existence*. With that understanding, if you are clear to here, do you have any questions before proceeding?"

"I do not," she confirmed.

"Then let's begin. We left off where you've arrived at the realm of Creation. This is where you and others are waiting to have a soul experience created for you. Also present are the Omniscient Divines, the most awakened souls in all of existence. Additionally, They are Those who are responsible for all existing, from the realm of Creation to where Humanity currently lives."

"Okay, that means…" Gail looked around the room, "the Omniscients, Those who live here, are the ones who created everything that exists outside of the *All that IS*?"

"Yes, to Humanity's experience, They created it all… every space, place, and soul that exists within the multi-realm Universe. Inclusive of, *the numerous realms…*" I overstated, for her benefit, "that are located within that Universe. And these credentials, Gail," I said, due to her previous reaction, "are why *They* are assisting you with your pending soul creation."

"What?" Gail's head reeled from where she was looking. "Multi-realm Universe? Numerous realms? Tell me their names, please!"

"Yes, numerous!" I laughed, knowing this was exciting news for her. "Though," I added, "it's not time to discuss them yet."

"Come on…" Gail sighed. "You're a tease."

"I know," I winked, "soon enough. For now, we'll proceed with your previous fascination, the creation of your soul."

"Okay, fine…" She easily conceded. "What happens next? Now that we've all located to the realm of Creation?"

"Well, after arriving, you have choices to make. First, will you exist to serve, or will you decide to have a soul's life experience? When that decision is made, you'll meet with the Omniscients to discuss where you will live. If you choose to serve, the Omniscients will decide where you are needed most."

"Hmm…" Gail squinted, thinking about it, then asked, "If a soul doesn't choose a life of service, how do they know which of the realms to consider living in?"

"One knows which to choose because they go through a very mindful, detailed decision-making process with the Omniscients. Which, in turn, highlights all possibilities or implications involved with one's choices."

"Implications? Are there unfavorable ones?"

"No, not really," I shook my head. "Not until things were turned upside down in Humanity's realm. Until then, if there were any matters to consider, they only revolved around what kind of experience one would like to have. As the further away one lives from the realm of Truth, the more interesting things can get."

"How so?" she asked.

"Well, one can experience lesser degrees of consciousness. Also, they may recall fewer Truths than other souls. Though that's true, every soul living beyond Humanity's experience always has access to and remains connected in their incepting Truths. And because they do," I emphasized, "that means they've never forgotten every soul's birthright and eternal intention, *which is to live and exist only in peace evermore.*"

"Okay, if I understand you correctly, you're saying all souls, except Humanity's, coexist in peace no matter where they live?"

"That's correct."

"Because they remember, understand, and can easily access their collective Truths?"

"Yes."

"That means..." Gail looked hopeful while calculating the facts, "when we deliver these Truths to Humanity, and they awaken with clearly understanding them, peace will be their default experience. That's one of the reasons why you are so certain Humanity can achieve peace?"

"It is! And…" I furthered her understanding, "the other reason I know peace is possible, is because the souls of Humanity share the exact same intention. Therefore, from the moment of their collective inception, *living in peace was the only way Humanity ever intended to live.*"

"Wow," Gail gazed at me, "*Truth, Clarity, and Hope* incoming…"

"That's right. And," I flashed a giant smile, "I'm planning to send a lot more doses of those each your way.

"Speaking of which…" I reached for the white binder.

Gail squeezed her hands together, closed her eyes tight, and chanted, "Please, please, please tell me the names of the realms."

Excited to do so, I thumbed through the papers I had placed before me to find the handout I had created.

"Yes!" Gail leaped out of her seat, assuming I would fulfill her wish.

"Yet…" I raised my hand, putting her on hold for a moment, "before I share the names of the realms, I need you to understand I've named them in how I know them, from the perspective of how I see and interpret them. Therefore, others may describe them differently. Though true, I assure you their energetic composition, vibrational frequency, and sequential order are accurately accounted for."

Gail nodded, then impatiently signaled for me to continue.

"Therefore, without further ado…" I placed the illustration before her, "here are the realms organized in descending order."

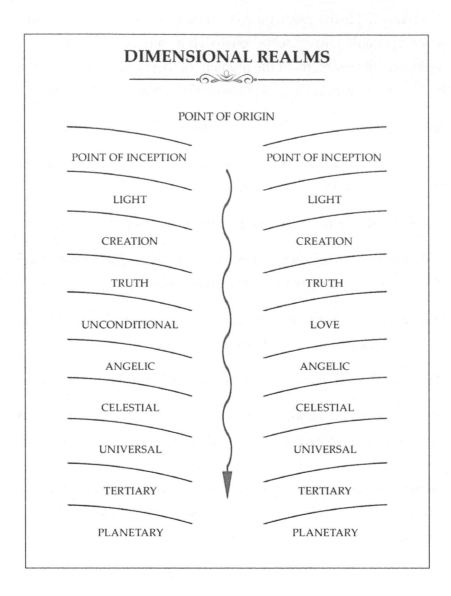

DIMENSIONAL REALMS

POINT OF ORIGIN

POINT OF INCEPTION — POINT OF INCEPTION

LIGHT — LIGHT

CREATION — CREATION

TRUTH — TRUTH

UNCONDITIONAL — LOVE

ANGELIC — ANGELIC

CELESTIAL — CELESTIAL

UNIVERSAL — UNIVERSAL

TERTIARY — TERTIARY

PLANETARY — PLANETARY

(Dear Reader: visit www.MyCallingMyQuest.com to download a more readable illustration in a free PDF format. This includes all handouts within this book.)

Gail reviewed the handout and then jumped to her feet again. This time though, to give me and the realms both standing ovations!

"Okay, okay! That's enough, silly girl..." I blushed.

Gail calmed herself and then reviewed the document again. When she was complete, she said, "Many on Earth say there are 12 realms. You only named 11."

"Yes, there are 12 in total. However, in the sequential order of how Humanity came into existence, the 12th doesn't exist yet."

"Okay..." Gail paused, looking at the realm handout again. "So, what I'm looking at is the multi-realm Universe, minus Humanity's realm?"

"No, what you are looking at are *all locations* existing outside of Humanity's realm."

"So, this is not the multi-realm Universe?" She pointed to the realms displayed.

"That's correct, it is not. Though true, the multi-realm Universe is shown within this illustration. It's comprised of the realms of *Truth, Unconditional Love, Angelic, Celestial, Universal, Tertiary, and Planetary.* These in total are what I call the *All that Exists.*"

"The *All that Exists*?"

"Yes. It's the place where all souls go to live post their creations. It's also the place where everyone created prior to Humanity's experience lives."

"You're referring to everything existing beneath the realm of Creation, right?"

"Yes. All of which is of the Omniscients' domain, dominion, and sole creation. And understand," I looked at Gail, "this diagram not only excludes Humanity's realm, but it also excludes the Universe they built-out for themselves."

"What?" Gail's eyebrows took rise. "Humanity has their own Universe?"

"They do, we'll discuss that later. For now, let's continue our current discussion."

She gave me two thumbs up, so I proceeded.

"Okay, we've reached the place where it's time for you and other *beings of Light* to address the choices before you. First, will you choose to serve or not? Next, where will you go to live? When decided, you each depart for the realm in which you've chosen to live. Or, if you choose to serve, you'll proceed to where the Omniscients need your assistance."

"If we choose to serve, where are we located?" she asked.

"Typically," I answered, "you are sent to one of the realms designated for service purposes only. They are the ones located directly below the realm of Creation. And those realms are…" I pointed to them on the handout, "Truth, Unconditional Love, Angelic, and Celestial. Well…" I corrected myself, "Celestial is a mix of both, which indicates some souls serve from there, and others have life experiences."

"I'm confused." Gail studied the realms. "Are we created before we are sent to our home realms?"

"Yes…" I laughed, "I guess I forgot to mention that."

"You did," she laughed too. Then she asked, "What were we made of?"

"You were created in likeness to the Omniscient Divines, and formed from the same substance and consciousness as They were."

"Which was?"

"The consciousness and matter existing within the *All that IS*." I referred to the *Order of Creation* handout I had placed before us. "Therefore, you were created *of the Light* and *its* consciousness. That is, when the Omniscients created you as a soul, They gleaned all resources needed from *the Light* itself."

"Whoa…" was all she said, nodding her head up and down. I gave her a moment, then asked if she had any questions.

"I do." She looked at me. "Is there anything you can share besides how all souls came into existence? For instance, can you speak to what a soul's life experience is like, for those who don't choose to serve?"

"I can, because…" I lingered, knowing she would love this, "I peeked in to understand how souls live and exist."

"Really? What did you see?"

"Well…" I thought about what to share, then answered. "The first thing I noticed was that after the souls had settled into their home realms, they remained within those locations only, rather than traveling or moving about the dimensions. I also saw that intermingling between souls from different realms initially was non-existent. This intrigued mc, with all there was to explore and experience."

"Was it because they weren't allowed to?"

"No, they could, but they didn't," I answered. "Because from what I saw, they were content with their new life experiences. It was more than obvious the souls were thoroughly enjoying the destinations they'd located to. And it appeared there was no reason or rising desire within them for it to be otherwise. Instead, I only felt the immense gratitude they had for all gifted to them."

"What else did you see?" Gail leaned in, eyes bright with curiosity.

"I saw that all souls have stunning ethereal-bodies filled with *the Light*. This leaves them with not having to contend with the physical, mental, spiritual, or consciousness issues existing on Earth. I also saw souls interacting, forming bonds, and having relationships similar to Humanity. Of course, minus the difficulties, disconnects, and fear-filled interactions experienced on Earth. And, Gail, most importantly, I discovered that fear is nonexistent beyond Humanity's experience."

"No fear? Anywhere?" Gail locked her eyes with mine.

"That's correct, none. Know though, I did see that some realms have conditions to work through, figure out, and resolve. But it's not because they veiled or isolated themselves from their support systems… *the Light*, the *All that IS*, the realm of Truth, and the Omniscients. Instead, it's because the locations where they live have them distanced from those resources."

"Amazing… how awesome it must be to live fear-free."

I nodded an exaggerated yes, wholeheartedly agreeing.

"Do they have families like we do on Earth?"

"Absolutely! Multitudes of soul families exist throughout the realms. Not traditional moms and dads because souls don't give birth to other beings. Yet, they are families indeed. How amazing it was to see families living happily together, where everyone experiences nothing less than pure adoration for one another."

Gail quieted, seeming to enjoy the insights revealed. I paused, too, so she could experience how she initially lived. How we all once lived. In time, she asked if there was anything else I could share.

"Well…" I considered, "there is something that's of great importance. And that is, all souls within all the realms have never forgotten they are members of the collective of *One*. If one's situation has them distanced from that knowing, it's of no issue.

"That's because," I continued, "the Omnipotent Divine and its consciousness keep them eternally aligned in that understanding. Also, because Truth is always within everyone's reach, no matter where they live. Truths inclusive of…" I playfully baited Gail, "what may exist beyond the Point of Origin."

"There's something beyond the Point of Origin?" Her eyes lit up.

"Maybe…" I shrugged and smiled. "From what I've seen, all things are possible. I'm not certain, though, since that's the furthest I was placed."

"Placed?" She tilted her head. "In the Point of Origin?"

"Yes, placed. Meaning, when it was time for me to gather Humanity's Truths, I was taken to that location."

"How did you get there?"

"Honestly, I don't know. I didn't ask."

Gail rolled her eyes, seeming to question my lack of curiosity.

"I know…" I shrugged a shoulder, "it's just how I am. Yet understand that initially, I was so confused and shocked, I didn't think to ask."

"So, tell me what happened." She turned to face me.

"Well, it happened when I was on the phone with Gwen, who was assisting me with documenting my discoveries. We were chatting away… then the next thing I knew, I was sitting at the Point of Origin with no forewarning."

"No one told you they were taking you there?"

"They did not. However, I know the benefit of that now. It's because it allowed me to understand Humanity's highest Truths without anything influencing my perception. And since you asked, I can see it was the Omniscients who placed me there."

"Way tooooo cool…" Gail gushed. "When did it happen? What was it like? Is it true? Can you show me where you were placed?"

"Yes, I can show you!" I laughed at her string of run-on questions. Then I suggested we relocate to the far end of the room to continue our discussion. Gail instantly agreed, jumped up from her chair, and headed down-room toward the *All that IS* without me. I knew she would need supervision, so I retrieved my notes and the white binder, and then quickly followed behind her.

Chapter 16

It's One for All, as All Are One

Arriving at the far end of the room, Gail immediately planted herself front and center to all I had opened to her previously. Not wanting her to take a deep dive head-first into the beyond physically, I positioned myself next to her. After all, we had a mutual quest to achieve, and it would be waylaid for weeks if I had to go chasing after her.

Knowing she would want answers to her questions immediately, I decided to address those first. When complete, I would transition us into the remainder of what I was to share before our return to Planet Earth.

"Okay, Gail," I began, "you want me to show you where I was placed within the Point of Origin, correct?"

"I do," she answered, while fidgeting.

"It was here." I reached up and pointed to the outermost, northeast corner of our view.

"And to answer your other questions, yes, I was taken to that location to retrieve the highest Truths of all. It was August 2014, eight months after Humanity had set their Third Intention.

"As far as what it was like?" I looked back at Gail. "It was spectacular! It was also confusing and overwhelming. I had absolutely no idea where I was since I was placed in the middle of non-existence and left there to figure it out," I laughed, because that is exactly what had happened.

"Can anyone else go there?" She shuffled closer to the edge of our view.

"I'm sure they could if their consciousness could withstand it." I reached over to limit her advancement.

"Is there anything else you can share about realm-life?" She finally settled in alongside me.

"Hmm… nothing more detailed than I have," I shook my head, "because I closed my investigation after finding the Truths I was looking for. However, one day I would love to explore the multi-realm Universe more thoroughly."

"Can I join you? Please?" she asked, ever so sweetly.

"Absolutely…" I answered, and then, knowing there was more to cover, I moved us forward. First, with bringing *The Making of You* conversation full-circle.

"Okay, Gail, in closing on the topic of souls and realms, understand that even though each dimension has its own activities, ways of living, established soul-families, and distinct domestic groupings, everyone still considers all souls existing as members of their lineage. This has never changed, nor will it ever, because all souls can easily access Truth no matter where they live.

"The outcome," I continued, "is everyone who lives in the multi-realm Universe operates, cooperates, and collectively exists cohesively. Therefore," I emphasized, "all dimensions beyond Humanity's existence are eternally linked and synched in peace, *the Light*, and the understandings of whom they are in Truth."

"Hmm…" she considered, then summed the premise for herself. "All are *One*, aligned in Truth, with no degree of separation."

"Exactly. And know, Gail, Humanity can have these experiences too. All they must do is embrace their Truths and awaken with them. When complete, they can then claim their true legacy and Divine inheritance… *to live in peace always and evermore.*"

Since this was the perfect lead-in for our next topic, I stepped forward and dropped the lowest draping—curtain number three. It hung horizontally, and after it was opened, it revealed all existing except where Humanity lives. This now allowed us to view all locations from the Point of Origin through the Planetary dimensional realm.

"Oh…" Gail softly gasped, with all that I had opened to her. She then held her palms facing forward, closed her eyes, and said, "It feels timeless, immense, expansive… familiar, welcoming, yet foreign. It seems so far-away… yet it's a very part of me. And…" she scooted closer, "from within it, I can sense the Truth of us all."

I quietly stood with Gail, wanting her to experience all existing beyond Humanity's realm. After much time, she reached over to hold my hand—I believe to anchor herself. She then gently reached into the multi-realm Universe to enhance her experience.

When complete, she stepped back and asked, "If all souls existing were created in likeness to the *All that IS*, representing it in matter, consciousness, and intention… then this is the reality of who every human being is, right?"

"Yes, it is…" I smiled, with her accurate summation.

"Then how odd it is," she squinted, looking to me, "so many on Earth believe the complete opposite. Humans believing other humans are less than, inferior, and worthless. Then, because they believe these things, they hate and harm one another. It makes no sense…" Gail shook her head, and then she turned to face all existing again.

"You are correct, it doesn't. Because all before you *IS* who *everyone* is in Truth, no matter where they live."

"That means…" Gail paused, "the Truths you share, the ones we'll deliver, can resolve Humanity's issues. Then, one day they can live like all souls do in the multi-realm Universe, in peace and harmony."

"Yes, Gail, one day they can live in peace again, with knowing the Truths of whom they are," I reaffirmed.

Then, with feeling the effects of our proximity to the *All that IS* myself, I led Gail to the chairs positioned behind us. When seated, I asked her to summarize all displayed within our view to make sure she understood everything presented so far.

"Well…" her expression was contemplative, "there's the Point of Origin, the Point of Inception, the realm of *Light*, the realm of Creation, *the Light* itself, Truth, *beings of Light*, and the Omniscients.

"Also," she continued, being more than thorough, "souls living happy, peaceful life experiences, souls who are serving, all goings-on and happenings within each realm, and the 'Omnipotent Divine' whom you mentioned earlier… whoever that is."

I chuckled because I had assumed she had missed my earlier introduction of that Divine. I then waited for the question I sensed was coming.

"So, is the Omnipotent Divine another God?" Gail teased me.

"No, not another God. Just another reason why Humanity and *you*," I teased her in return, "gets worked up about what the Divine is or is not. Maybe this will help," I pulled a summary from the white binder and held it before her.

THE ORDER OF SOURCE

THE ALL THAT IS
aka the Omnipotent Divine

The *All that IS*, also known as the Omnipotent Divine, is *the Light* and *the Light* is *its* consciousness. It is that which affords all who exist the opportunity to come into existence. It is also that which inspired us each to exist as souls. Its consciousness— *the One Divine Mind*—is our highest consciousness, and that consciousness is the highest source of support we can utilize to sustain our wellbeing.

THE OMNISCIENT DIVINES

The Omniscient Divines, firstly, are the most conscious souls in all of existence. They are also the *Divine Creators* who gave all *beings of Light* the opportunity to exist as souls. Additionally, They are the ones who created all existing within the multi-realm Universe. Although, They are not the ones who created what exists within the realm of Humanity. Currently, there are seven serving within the realm of Truth, as the eighth has relocated.

(**Dear Reader: visit www.MyCallingMyQuest.com to download a more readable illustration in a free PDF format. This includes all handouts within this book.**)

"Okay," she looked at me after her review, "I think I understand the definition of the *All that IS* and the Omnipotent Divine now, but *who* is it exactly?"

"Technically, Gail, the Omnipotent Divine is not a *who*, it's a *what*. Though true, know it is *who* every being, soul, and person is. Yet, in Truth…" I smiled widely, loving the mystery of this Truth, "it is actually *no one* at all."

"Okay…" Gail squinted, piecing together what I had shared. Then she summed her understanding. "It's similar to when we became *the Light*? We existed, yet we were not a *someone* yet?"

"Yes! That's an excellent example. And don't forget, before that, you were a portion of the *All that* IS even though you did not exist yet."

"Hmm…" She thought about it. "Maybe that's why some people believe we are each individually the Divine."

"Possibly…"

Gail nodded and asked, "Can I try summing this topic? To know if I understand it clearly?"

"Absolutely."

"Okay," Gail began. "On Earth right now, there's a lot of confusion about *what* or *who* the Divine is. Especially around the topic of… G-o-d," she spelled it out, whispering.

I laughed at her attempt to adhere to our beliefs agreement.

She then continued, saying, "Some people believe there is only *one Being* who created all of existence. Those people also believe that *one Being* is the *only Being* who oversees the wellbeing of everything. Others, though, believe it's not an *individual Being* or a *who*. Instead, for them, it's a *what*... most commonly called *the Universe* or *Source*.

"In the end, though, it's both!" Gail thrilled over her discovery. "Because the Omniscients, including Humanity's own, are the *who*. And, the *All that IS* as the Omnipotent Divine is the *what*. Now I clearly understand why Humanity is continuously confused with this topic, why the debating never ends."

"Well said!" I celebrated her understanding. "And it's that confusion as to why it was decided Humanity would more easily awaken with their Truths versus their beliefs. Because once they understand the *big picture* of who they are, they can finally lay their confusion and hostilities to rest."

"I'm starting to understand that peace really is possible through these disclosures." Gail inhaled deeply. "How Humanity's grievances with each other are resolvable with their Truths and *the Awakening Plan*."

"Yes. It's all possible," I confirmed.

"And Gail," I approached curtain number three, then dropped it to the floor and pointed to Planet Earth, "Truth and this *Awakening Plan* are not the only reasons I know peace is possible, since thousands upon thousands have come to Earth to help Humanity reach peace. It's why you, I, and others are serving as we do, and it's the only reason why we exist.

"I also know peace is achievable," I continued, "because Humanity's Awakening and conscious ascent are now Universal goals supported on Earth and beyond as never before."

"If that's true," Gail stood and joined me, "then why does Humanity believe their needs and pleas for assistance go unnoticed? Believe no one's attempting to help? That no one cares?"

"It's because of the fallout from their Second Intention. As we know, though," I traced an imaginary circle around everything displayed before us, "the Truth is, everyone existing beyond Earth cares tremendously, since it's *One* for all, as all are *One*, eternally evermore.

"Therefore," I highlighted, "when any being, soul, or realm is out of balance, lost, confused, or compromised, the collective of *One* does everything possible to assist. This includes what's happening on Earth currently."

"Wow, that's powerful!" She shivered. "I'll remind Humanity of these Truths time and time again until they feel and know them as Truth too. Also, so that they can clearly understand that no one has abandoned or forgotten about them."

"Please do, as the love, assistance, and commitment from all dimensions and realms will never end. We will not walk away or stop offering our services until our total soul family is aligned and living as *One* again. And these commitments, coupled with Humanity setting their Third Intention to awaken, are the final reasons I know peace is possible."

Gail looked to me, wide-eyed, with tears falling down her cheeks.

I gave her a nod, a smile too, letting her know there was hope for Humanity.

She then turned to face existence in total again, and whispered, "Peace on Earth is possible… because it's *One* for all, as all are *One*, eternally evermore."

"Truth, pure Truth…" I whispered as well, so as not to affect her experience.

I then fell silent so that Gail could spend time with some of the most important Truths she would ever encounter and teach. While doing so, I received a nudge from the Omniscients. They informed me it was time for us to end our visit and return to Earth since Gail had received all Truths I was to share within this realm. It was also time to depart for Gail's highest wellbeing. After all, she had spent more time within our realm than anyone else had, other than those assigned to serve within it. With that knowing, I leaned toward Gail and suggested a change of scenery.

"Where?" She looked at me.

"Planet Earth, because that's where we are to discuss *how Humanity came into existence.*"

"Do we have to?"

"We do."

"Okay…" she sighed.

Gail then turned, closed her eyes, and affectionately reached out one final time to experience the *All that IS* as though it were her last time.

In appreciation for her affection, the *All that IS* wrapped itself around her with the most loving embrace I have ever witnessed. This emotionally brought me to my knees, with my eternal soul's purpose now showing itself to me.

With an outpouring of energetic intensity now consuming both Gail and me, They reminded me the time to leave was Now! In full agreement, I leaned toward Gail and asked if she was ready to go. Next, without allowing her time to answer, I took her by the hand and aimed for Humanity's realm.

After arriving to my earthly home, I turned to see how Gail had faired on our journey. To my delight, she was well, which she confirmed with a giant smile. We then both giggled from the excitement of traveling from one dimension to another.

"Wow, that was incredible!" Gail beamed, while rattling her head back and forth. "We visited the realm of Truth! Who would've thought such a thing existed?"

I laughed, happy she had loved the experience.

"Where do we go from here?"

"Well…" I considered, "we'll need to take some downtime before meeting again since you will need to reacclimate to the conditions on Earth. Then, when we resume, we'll continue with the account of Humanity's existence. Does that work?"

"Yes," she answered, "let's meet in three weeks because I have some things I need to tend to. And strangely enough…" she yawned, "I'm feeling the effects of returning already."

"Then let's call it a day," I offered.

Gail nodded, turned to face me, and then she embraced me in the same fashion as the *All that IS* had embraced her—with endless love and appreciation.

"Thank you for taking me to the realm of Truth," she whispered to me, "and for the Truths we so desperately need."

Grateful for our experience as well, I relaxed and leaned into Gail's warmth and endearments. I then sent great thanks of my own to Those beyond for everything accomplished with our visit. Most importantly, *the highest Truths of whom every being is* were now successfully received and delivered.

When our moment concluded, Gail took both of my hands into hers, and said, "I'm so honored to serve with you, and I want you to know I will do so until the end of time. And," she locked her eyes with mine, possibly knowing my oncoming thoughts, "there is nothing from the Point of Origin to where we stand together today that can ever change that."

"Thank you." I smiled, hoping it would prove true, despite returning to where fear was residing. Not wanting to park on that reality yet, I reminded myself of the strides we had made, and that we were already far down the path of her receiving the *Awakening Plan for Peace*.

Knowing it was time to part ways, we embraced one final time. Then, as she set off, I noticed she was not the same Gail I had taken to the realm of Truth. Her appearance was now showing a lightness increasing within, her already thin veil was visibly fading, and there was an incredible peace weaving its essence throughout her entirety. All of which had clearly resulted from… her consciousness rising with her understanding of Truth.

"Imagine that…" I said to myself, "this plan works."

Of course, I believed in its ability to help Humanity awaken. Yet, to watch it unfold with Gail's transformation was proof of all it could accomplish. I took a deep breath, grateful for the confirmation, and felt excitement rise for the day when Gail returned. The day when Humanity would be one step closer to aligning with all existing beyond their realm. The result would be not one single member of our total soul family would have to experience anything not of peace, *the Light*, and the loving embrace of the *All that IS* ever again.

Chapter 17

The Founders of Humanity

In early August, on the day Gail was returning, my whole body was pulsing, on-point, and teeming with enthusiasm. How could it not? Since I would finally get to share the additional Truths I had found regarding *how Humanity themselves came into existence*. Truths that were equally noteworthy and fascinating to how all conscious beings and souls first incepted.

Noteworthy, because few on Earth are entirely familiar with the origins of their collective experience. Fascinating, because of the phenomenal orchestrations, agreements, and relationships resulting from Humanity setting their First Intention.

Beyond motivated to start my day, I got straight to work reviewing the material we would cover. This I did minus my usual morning cup of coffee because the Mortal Majority's elations for what I would share next were frenetically cresting! When my review was complete, I organized my notes, and just as I was finishing… I felt a wave of enthusiasm press into my home. Certain that it was for Gail's arrival, I stood to greet her as she approached.

"Hi!" she said, while wrapping her highly-charged excitement around me, which was so energetically intense we had to immediately release our embrace!

She then stepped away and attempted to shake off the effects of our moment with a purposeful, full-body shiver. She followed that by saying, "I feel like I drank a gallon of espresso!"

"Right!" I agreed, grateful I had passed on my strongly brewed, homemade concoction.

Then, with wanting her to understand the full scope of our moment, I said, "You know, Gail, the intensity of what we are experiencing is not only due to our excitement, it's also inclusive of the Mortal Majority's."

Gail looked at me, tilting her head. "The souls of Humanity?"

"Yes. They've anxiously awaited this moment because they believe the Truths shared today will pave the way for the fulfillment of Humanity's Third Intention. They also believe these Truths are the ones Humanity needs most to achieve peace."

"Okay…" Gail lingered, looking about the room. "From what I remember, we'll be discussing how Humanity came into existence, right?"

"Yes."

"Then I assume you'll share similar Truths to those shared on Earth already, by telling the same story everyone tells. The one about how everything was created. If so, what's the significance? Because other than how that story is told, there's little difference."

"It matters because," I smiled, knowing its significance, "the account shared today is fully intact. Meaning, it's not missing Truths that were withheld, nor is it lacking Truths many on Earth have forgotten."

Gail quieted, then delayed thoughtfully for several moments. When finished, looking overly worried, she asked, "So the creation story told on Earth isn't true?"

"It is true. However, most versions don't account for the entirety of how, when, and why Humanity incepted. For instance, who were the visionaries behind a new dimension coming into existence? Why does Humanity live in separation from *All that Exists*? And just how did they get a life experience unto themselves only?"

"Oh..." she relaxed, "I guess the *whole story* clarity I am seeking just multiplied a thousand-fold."

"And even more so..." I confirmed.

The Mortal Majority then connected and insisted we get on with it! To honor their request, I asked Gail, "Are you ready to begin?"

"More than," she answered, while taking a seat on the sofa.

"Perfect. Three weeks ago," I began, while glancing at my notes, "before returning from the realm of Truth, we discussed how all who exist came into existence. That portion of Humanity's account is considered as *Act One*. Today, we'll discuss *Act Two* and *Act Three*, starting with a brief review of what we've already discussed."

Gail interrupted, "Can I help? By summing what I remember?"

"Absolutely. Go for it," I encouraged.

"Let's see…" Gail looked out the window as though she were tracking and mapping the events herself. "A long time ago, at the Point of Origin, where nothing yet exists… we have a burning desire to come into existence as the *All that IS*. Our desire then presses us forward, to a place named the Point of Inception… and when we arrive, we are *the Light*, which means we now exist!" she enthused, then looked back at me with an adorable, wily smile.

"Oh… my… goodness!" I laughed at her well-rehearsed rendition. "You used our time apart effectively."

Gail nodded, smiling ear to ear, then continued her summation.

"We've arrived, we became *the Light*, and guess what happens next?"

I shrugged, playing along.

"Our desires take rise…" she pointed upward, "which carries us forward, so now we exist in consciousness. *Beings of Light* are who we are, and our home is called the realm of *Light*. Peace and happiness are our only experiences, and we live this way for eternities… until the day we consciously decide to exist in yet another way. This, of course," Gail winked at me, "is how it plays out because our desire brings it about.

"Then we migrate to the realm of Creation," she continued, "which is where the Omniscients are waiting to receive us. After that, to our delight, They graciously create our soul life experiences. When complete, They disperse us each, throughout the numerous realms. And it's there we live, within *All that Exists* until we become Humanity!" Gail excited, concluding her summation.

"Yay!" I cheered for her creativeness.

"You know," Gail said, while blushing from my accolades, "there seems to be a pattern in how all things come into existence, with *desire* being the key ingredient."

"Yes ma'am, as from the Point of Origin to the place where we stand on Planet Earth, desire is how all existing comes about. After all," I added, "we are instinctually inclined by our unending desire to exist in yet another way."

Clearly understanding, Gail concluded my premise. "Because from the moment we incept at the Point of Origin, it's of our nature to endlessly express ourselves as an essence of the *All that IS.*"

"Truth!" I concurred. Then, with her impeccable clarity, I asked if she would like to advance Humanity's story herself. Of course, she instantly agreed!

"All right…" Gail began again. "Souls were happy and all was well within the multi-realm Universe. Then…" she looked away, "something happened after their desire took rise…" she lingered, seeming unsure where to go next.

"You've got this," I encouraged her.

"Okay…" She closed her eyes and tried again. "The soul's desires took rise again, and then…" she stopped, opened her eyes, and looked to me. "Help please, I'm unsure what happened before they became Humanity."

Happy to assist, I picked up from there, in likeness to her clever rendition.

"Something happened that had never happened or was ever considered before. Humanity's Founders from the realm named Love came up with the most brilliant, exceptional idea of all. Which was…" I paused, dramatically, "they as eight, took to the ethers to travel throughout the dimensional realms!"

"Realm-traveling?" Gail's eyes opened wide. "Take me, please!"

I laughed, shaking my head, and then continued.

"The Founders ascended, then they descended, and conquered the greatest challenges of all. And because they did, they gained 'Rockstar' status, resulting in thousands tagging along. Of course, the Founders welcomed one and all so they could have fantastic experiences too! And obviously, eventually… they bonded, became family, and vowed their allegiance to explore together, now and evermore."

Gail piped in, "They loved and adored their new life experience, most likely for eternities. Then one day, as before, their desire took rise again."

"Yes, yet, that was not until…" I backtracked us, "they had finished pressing the limits of their conscious abilities. When complete, they longed for more, and though they wanted more…" I lingered for effect, "what they wanted most was a place of their own they could call home."

"Aw…" Gail touched her heart with her palm, "that was unexpected."

I nodded, smiled, and resumed. "Traveling the realms then gave way to them planning and detailing for what they wanted next. Once they finished, they asked to meet with the incredible Omniscient Divines.

And that was when they ambitiously requested a whole new realm be created for them."

"Whoa…" Gail raised her eyebrows to the beyond. "The Founders went to the Omniscients directly? Then they asked for a realm of their own?"

"They did. And on top of that," I announced next, "they also asked for abilities to create in likeness to Them."

"In likeness to the Omniscients?" Gail's eyes opened wider than before.

"Yes."

"Well… those are the bravest, boldest requests I've ever heard!"

"Agreed," I nodded, and then I finished the summation of *Act Two*. "The Omniscient Divines considered their requests, then graciously gave them their desired 'Yes.' That, of course, resulted in everyone present, including the Omniscients, melting into a giant love-fest!" I laughed because that is precisely what had happened.

"Seriously?" she asked. "Realm-traveled? Solicited the Omniscients? And asked to be creators too?"

"Yes, seriously. And know, Gail," I added, "despite their requests seeming presumptuous, it was their 'brave nature and bold requests' that expedited some of the most spectacular opportunities to have ever existed. Including the inception of Humanity themselves and all existing within their own Universe."

"Wow…" She moved her head back and forth. "The Founders are the most highly achieving, let's shoot for our highest potentials and goals souls I've ever heard of."

"They still are. And understand," I said, "meeting the highest benchmarks of all is what every human being is capable of equally. After all, they are the descendants and offspring of the Founders, who represent the Truth of who every member of Humanity is.

"Which shows," I highlighted, "that something seemingly impossible like reaching peace is a viable outcome because Humanity is capable of that and even more than that again."

"Amazing…" Gail trailed off, closing her eyes, while quietly whispering to herself. "Humanity's ancestors from beyond are who Humanity is… brave-bold-daring, capable of anything, including peace on Earth."

Gail then went silent, possibly delving into the opportunities before Humanity if they decided to ascend in consciousness. After numerous minutes of allowing her time to absorb what I had shared, I expressed a nuance of Humanity's story to her, hoping to draw her back to where we were heading.

"Once upon a time, in a far, far, far away place…" I whispered, "the Founders of Humanity took rise to explore the multi-realm lands. This then launched some of the most exciting and challenging ventures any soul has ever had."

Gail giggled and opened her eyes. "Yeah, even I have a burning desire to experience all that, especially realm-traveling. So, why's it so challenging?"

"It's challenging because each realm has its own consciousness that's uniquely calibrated to its location."

"Okay…" she considered, "and that means?"

"It means realm-traveling can be difficult. If a soul is unable to withstand or acclimate to the conscious conditions within any given realm, their visit will need to end. For instance, the closer a realm is to the realm of Truth, the higher degrees of consciousness one must acclimate to. Therefore, what it comes down to is whether one can tolerate high levels of Truth or not.

"In reverse, if one is descending through the realms, they'll need to contend with the effects of lesser degrees of consciousness, since they are equally difficult to adjust to. Either way, the challenge lies in one's ability to consciously acclimate to the location they're visiting. If unable, they must leave and rethink their approach. And the fun in it for everyone is figuring out how to master the entire process."

"I think I understand," Gail said. "Realm-traveling reminds me of the first time when people on Earth wanted to have underwater adventures. They had to figure out how to manage difficulties in pressurizing themselves with ascending and descending."

"Great example! Adjusting to fluctuations of consciousness within the realms is nearly the same. I know this because I both scuba-dive and realm-travel." I then laughed from a surfacing memory.

"What's so funny?"

"It has to do with scuba diving. The fact that the most peaceful place on Earth for me is located the furthest away from the realm of Truth. It's a location found deep within the caves of the cenotes in the Yucatan. Talk about peace beyond belief… I thought I'd been taken from Earth back to the realm of Truth because none of the issues here can press through into that blissful, beneath-the-water experience."

With that explained, I asked Gail if she had any questions before moving forward.

"I do. My first is, are the Founders still around? Are they of any importance now?"

"They are, and we'll discuss their importance when we cover how Humanity descended in consciousness."

"Okay," she readily accepted. "My next question is, can you share more about the exchanges that took place between the Founders and Omniscients? What happened overall?"

"Sure…" I paused, considering how to sum "what happened overall." When found, I began.

"We left off where the Founders and those who'd joined them had decided they wanted to have a brand-new life experience. What I'd highlight here is, all souls were beyond grateful for everything initially created and gifted to them. Yet, after they had mastered all challenges found within the Universe they lived, they went searching for something new to experience once again."

"So…" Gail participated, "they solicited the Omniscients and asked to be given more to appease their desires."

"Correct. Yet," I said, "the souls did not approach the Omniscients until they had constructed a detailed, well-considered plan. When complete, and with their request to meet granted, all wanting to participate were asked to proceed to the Universal dimensional realm."

"Why there?"

"Because that realm was conducive to everyone's conscious abilities. Therefore, no one would have an issue with acclimating to that destination."

"That makes sense," she nodded.

"Perfect," I said, and then continued. "After arriving, all souls gathered before the Omniscients. Then, their selected representatives, the original eight who'd instigated realm traveling, explained the details of their collective request. First, they wanted to have an additional life experience created for them. In other words, they wanted to exist and take form in yet another way.

"Additionally," I added, "they wanted to live far from all existing. This would allow them to have exciting explorations together, 'uniquely only available to them.' Finally, as mentioned, they wanted the opportunity to create in likeness to the Omniscients."

"Amazing..." Gail slowly rocked her head side to side, "I still can't believe they asked for that."

"I know..." I thoroughly agreed, and then I continued.

"What happened next was the Omniscients discussed the Founder's requests amongst Themselves. Then, as said, They gave Their answer of 'Yes.' After that, They promised They would create the most exceptional, unimaginable experience found anywhere within all of existence. With that conveyed, the Omniscients then discussed the finer details in how to fulfill the souls' requests. When decided, They created a space, place, and realm for the souls to call home just South of the multi-realm Universe."

"So cool…" Gail's eyes shined bright. "Imagine a whole new realm created for you. What did they name it?"

"The Founders asked their new home be named *Love*," I answered. "First, to honor where they were from, the initial realm of Love, which was where love first incepted. Second, because they hoped their new home, as their former, would exemplify the highest love of all. Lastly, they asked it be named *Love* for all they were gifted. With the most valuable gift being the up-close, personal time they were afforded to spend with the Omniscients."

"Aw…" she cooed, "I imagine so. After all, how many souls get the opportunity to meet with Them all?"

"Very few. Most souls never cross paths with an Omniscient past their souls' creation."

"What happened next?"

"Well, those who attended, including the Omniscients, melted into the giant love-fest I mentioned. This then gave rise… to one of the greatest exchanges of love I have ever witnessed, anywhere within all of existence."

"Please explain 'love-fest,' " Gail requested. "What's the importance?"

"It's meaningful because the Omniscients were experiencing love as They had never experienced it before."

Gail scooted to the edge of the sofa. "They had not encountered love before?"

"No, not really," I shook my head. "At least not the personification of it."

"I'm confused. How is this the first time the Omniscients experienced love?"

"Um…" I paused, unsure of how to respond. After finding my way, I answered, "It's due to where They live."

"Still confused." She squinted, trying to make the connection.

"Remember when we discussed realm-traveling?" I asked. "And I mentioned how each realm consists of a calibrated consciousness conducive to where it's located?"

"Yes."

"Well, that basis also lends to one's life experience being contingent on where one lives. So, for the Omniscients who reside in the realm of Truth, which is above the realm of Love, They rarely, if ever, were exposed to love as a consciousness. That's because the only existing consciousnesses They had interfaced with to this occasion were *the Light* and Truth."

"This is so interesting…" Gail thought about it.

When she had assimilated all shared, she said, "That means this was the first time the Omniscients experienced love as an action, exchange, and personal endearment."

"That's correct," I slowly nodded, "and They were so taken with it, They returned the love They'd received to Their fullest capacities. The outcome was, everyone present was swept away into an epic flood of love."

"Whoa…" Gail softly gasped, looking to the beyond. "I imagine so, because Their collective consciousness and its effects are massive."

"Exactly. Hence, as said, it was the greatest exchange of love I have ever seen."

I then took a pause, with tears oncoming, because I could feel the magnitude of Humanity's defining moment. Wanting to conclude *Act Two* effectively, I inhaled and exhaled slowly. When I had centered myself, I continued.

"With intentions set, agreements made, and beautiful relationships founded in love for eternity, the Omniscients officially announced the new realm of Love was now a reality."

"Chills…" Gail shivered and inhaled deeply.

"Agreed…" I nodded. "And, Gail, chills equally for what happened next, since it's the single, most unselfish act of kindness I have ever witnessed. The Omniscients then collectively decided to indefinitely locate one of Their own to the furthest-away place from where They resided."

"Seriously?" Gail whispered. "An Omniscient left Their home?"

"Yes," I swiped a tear from my cheek, "They did. With the intention to love, care for, and oversee the wellbeing of Humanity for eternity."

"Oh…" was all she said, with her own tears now falling.

She then went silent, obviously moved by this Truth, as she shifted her gaze to the beyond. During her moment of silence, I took one as well to steady myself, so I would not emotionally falter with how deeply that Omniscient's commitment affected me. Once Gail had returned from where she was, she shared her thoughts with me.

"I never thought about where Humanity's Omniscient was from. Nor did I consider that an Omniscient gave up Their entire life experience. That They left behind those They loved and adored most, so Humanity could come into existence."

"I know… most people are not familiar with this Truth."

Gail looked at me, then locked her tear-filled eyes with mine, possibly to calm herself with everything she was feeling.

"What is it?" I asked, wanting to know.

"Well…" she replied, while wiping her tears away, "it's just that the Truths of Humanity's inception are the exact Truths I've been searching for. They're the ones needed most on Earth so that Humanity can understand that color, race, and sub-human classes are just fallacies.

"They're also the Truths," she continued, "that will help them recognize no matter where one lives… neighborhood, city, state, country, here, *There*, or beyond, that there are absolutely no dissimilarities as to who everyone is.

"Then with this information," she stated with confidence, "they'll know they are *One* from the moment they set their First Intention. Also know, they are capable of peace because they originated from *the greatest love of all*."

"Wow…" I uttered only, in response to Gail's perfected summation about the *power of Truth*.

She then whispered to herself and affirmed one final time, "Yes, the Truths in how all souls, beings, and Humanity themselves came into existence are the ones needed most on Planet Earth."

With her final affirmation, we were both emotionally swept away into all Humanity could achieve with the *Awakening Plan for Peace*.

After several minutes of lingering in that profound place with Gail, I pulled myself together and announced we were due for a break. Gail said she wanted to continue, but I informed her she would need time to acclimate to all Truths shared. She reluctantly agreed, yet admitted taking rest may benefit her. She then accepted my offer to relax at my home so that we could continue that day. I showed her to the guest room, where she laid on the bed, and then quickly drifted into a state of rest.

"Happy processing, dear Gail…" I whispered, closing the door behind me.

With Gail settled in, I returned to the living room and decided to take some downtime for myself. First, to reflect on the beautiful Truth-ride Gail and I had taken. Second, to temper the emotional effects of how deeply she had connected with Humanity's Truths. Last, so I could rest up for the remainder of what I was to disclose about how Humanity came into existence.

Though my downtime intention was to drift to sleep, sleep never fell upon me. However, taking some time for myself served my mind and body well. It also allowed me the opportunity to revel in the fact that the *Awakening Plan for Peace* was finally seeing the light of day within Humanity's realm.

Chapter 18

Love

Nearly two hours later, I decided to check in on Gail. I knocked lightly on the door, and with no reply, I entered and took a seat on the edge of the bed. To get her attention, I whispered her name several times until she slowly rolled toward me. After acknowledging my presence, I told her I would give her a few moments to herself, and then she could join me in the kitchen when ready.

"No, please stay," Gail stopped me. "I need to discuss the experience I just had."

"Okay," I replied, taking a seat on the floor. "What happened?"

"Well, first, I'm unsure if I was dreaming or not, which is probably irrelevant. Though…" she reconsidered, "I'm pretty sure it was real. Either way, shortly after I dozed off, I suddenly found myself somewhere other than Earth. I know this because I was amongst souls rather than humans."

Intrigued, I scooted closer toward the bed. That, in turn, prompted her to join me on the floor.

"Initially," Gail continued, while seating herself, "I was uncertain where I was. That is until I saw all souls present were having or have had life experiences on Earth. The point is, they were members of Humanity's collective. How did I know that?"

I nodded eagerly, wanting to know.

"I knew it because the souls were fixated on their human selves. Also, they were highly focused on the work you and I are doing together. Then, the next thing that happened was a soul approached and placed my hand into hers. It's a good thing she did," she giggled, "otherwise I might have been carried away into an endless abyss!"

"What happened?" I leaned in.

"A sea of souls, thousands and thousands, turned to face me. Then, they poured their beyond imaginable love onto me. It was so surreal…" Gail closed her eyes, inhaling deeply, "and by far the most breathtaking experience I've had in any retrievable memory.

"Until," her eyes popped open, "the soul holding my hand turned to face me and wrapped her infinite endearments around me. And because she did, I now know love as I've never known it before…" Gail lingered in her experience, while slowly rocking herself back and forth.

I sat quietly, understanding how meaningful her experience must have been, knowing it was hers to enjoy.

Several minutes later, she resurfaced and continued.

"I'm certain it was unconditional love because it filled and consumed my entire existence. I also know it because I have never encountered love so purely driven. I don't know," Gail shook her head, "my words pale to my experience. Yet, what I'm certain of is… she wanted me to understand what love *is*."

"And now, you know…" I reached out, gently touching her heart with my fingertips.

Gail gave a nod, with tears falling as she looked off into the distance.

"Are you okay?" I asked, sensing they were not happy tears.

"No, I'm not." She looked back toward me. "Because I don't understand why I've not experienced that kind of love before. I love everyone near and dear to my heart with all I am, and they love me the same. They're exceptional people, who have greater abilities to love unconditionally than most. However," she sighed, "our exchanges don't compare to what I just experienced. Why is that? Why is the love I felt *There* so foreign?"

"Because Gail," I sighed too, "love's abilities on Earth were compromised. Primarily because of the expectations and conditions people have placed on it. Like how love 'should be' shown, given, and expressed."

"I know that already." Gail looked down, lightly brushing the carpet with her fingers.

I nodded, knowing she did.

"It's probably why the first realm of Love had a name change," she mumbled, not looking up.

Not remembering mentioning that change, I asked how she knew that.

"Because the realm diagram you shared earlier noted the realm of Unconditional Love, not just Love."

"You are correct, Gail, that realm's name was changed because love on Earth no longer accurately expresses what love truly is."

With my confirmation, Gail slipped further into sadness.

Feeling for her realizations, I gently touched her hand with mine. "Gail, I'm sorry your heart hurts. Please understand, though, the love you just experienced is the only kind of love Humanity was ever supposed to know."

"What happened? Why's it this way?" Gail looked up, her eyes filled with pain.

"It's due to the Second Intention Humanity set. Which in the end," I sadly reported, "allowed fear to rule on Planet Earth, which diminished love's abilities forevermore. Well…" I paused, checking myself, "not forevermore, just until now. And Gail, fortunately, you and I are here to help remedy this situation."

"But if one tries really hard to reconnect with unconditional love beyond, they can experience that kind of love on Earth now too, right?"

"One could, yet few will."

"Why?" Her eyebrows knitted together.

"It's due to Humanity's Second Intention," I restated. "It's also due to Humanity veiling themselves as we discussed earlier. The result is that most on Earth are blocked from the love you just experienced. Know though," I added, hoping it would help, "some living on Earth do experience nothing less than unconditional love since it's their default experience."

"Who are they?"

"Well…" I thought about it, "like those of us who came in unveiled to serve. Unconditional love is our standard experience if we steer clear of the reality Humanity created."

"I came to serve, so why is this the first time I have experienced love this way?" Gail tossed her hands into the air.

"Because," I answered, "you arranged for it to be this way. You purposefully chose to experience life as Humanity does, for the benefit of helping them in the highest of ways."

"Right…" she sighed, dropping her head. After nursing her disappointment for not experiencing love as others had, she asked, "So the souls brought me there to understand what unconditional love is?"

"Um," I considered, then shook my head. "Instead, I think they called you there to thank you for the phenomenal progress we're making with landing their Truths. Therefore, your unconditional love experience was most likely a byproduct, not the purpose."

Gail agreed that was probably true. Yet, said it was of no consolation because unconditional love was so foreign to her. I assured her, one day, she would feel grateful for the experience she'd had. Then, as it appeared she was in a better place, I announced I had prepared lunch and would like to eat before getting back to work.

During the meal, which was unaccompanied by conversation, Gail remained fixated with her encounter beyond the veil. Knowing the fascinating Truths regarding Humanity's inception were awaiting us, I decided to engage, with hopes her disposition would shift.

"Gail," I reached out, "why are you still struggling?"

"Because my heart hurts for Humanity," she answered, through a stream of tears. "Since they've spent countless years on Earth without knowing the love I just experienced."

"I understand. We're all saddened by this," I exhaled, knowing the situation on Earth far too well. "Rest assured, though, one day all who live here will experience unconditional love again, I promise.

"Of course," I added, "it's Humanity's goal to achieve. Yet, it is achievable, especially…" I smiled, hoping to lift her spirits, "with us delivering the *Awakening Plan for Peace*."

"I hear you, yet if Humanity could feel that kind of love right now, then I'm certain they would do everything possible to live as they previously did. But," she exhaled, "it appears that's an impossibility on Planet Earth."

"Not true, Gail," I interrupted, "because Humanity can experience unconditional love right now… through you, me, and those who are not bound by the consciousness issues existing on Earth."

"Well, maybe they can experience it through you and others. However, no one's going to experience unconditional love through me if I've not experienced love like that before," she stated, sounding defeated.

"And," she added, "I obviously have a lot of work to do before I can benefit anyone."

"Oh, Gail…" I leaned across the table, taking her hands in mine. "Realize you're already quite advanced in your Awakening. You're almost there… because you've already transcended fear, the veil, and separation to greater degrees than most. And realize, you couldn't have experienced what you did if you weren't already far along your path."

"But you get to feel this kind of love every day." Gail pulled her hands away. "You're equally capable of giving it. So, you've practiced discipline, mindfulness, reverence, and dedication better than me." She dropped her eyes, looking ashamed.

"Not true," I adamantly stated. "And please don't compare yourself to me. It's unfair for you to do so with me living unveiled. And my goodness," I shared, remembering, "if you only knew what I went through to serve as I do today, you wouldn't be so hard on yourself. I've done this no better than you. In fact, less so."

Gail shook her head vigorously, showing she did not believe me.

"Unfortunately, it's true…" I looked away. "For many years before I found my way, I caused difficulties for many… chaos, confusion, and turning other's worlds upside down. I had no idea how to live, exist, cope, or manage my consciousness on Earth.

"That includes," I looked back at Gail, "how I have loved others since unconditional love is highly misinterpreted when shown and given. Trust me, Gail," I sighed, "I know your shame, I know your regret, and I know your pain for thinking you should have done better."

"You didn't do it on purpose, though," she countered. "And for that matter, you're living under extreme conditions on Earth. It's nothing like where you're from, therefore living here must have debilitating effects on you."

I raised both eyebrows for a full ten seconds, then said, "The extreme conditions on Earth have debilitating effects on everyone, not just on me. So please quit being so hard on yourself. And never forget," I suggested, hoping she would see the gifts of what she had perceived as her flaws, "it's through our shortcomings we will most effectively help others."

Gail sat quietly for a long time. Then, eventually, she acknowledged, though still unsmiling, she knew what I had shared was true.

With her understanding confirmed, and not wanting her to take a turn for the worse again, I leaned forward and pulled her into a loving embrace. I then reassured her she was well on her way to living as everyone had before the veil's placement. When complete, I asked if she would like to continue today. She answered yes, so I promised a topic to lift her mood—*Act Three, the Making of Humanity.*

Chapter 19

The Inception and Commencement of Humanity

Once I had finished tidying up after lunch, I asked Gail to join me in the living room. While seating myself, I noticed the room was filling with the comforting warmth of the afternoon sun. For many in Georgia, the sunshine and accompanying heat in August were unwelcome visitors. For me, though, with my home draped daylong beneath my oversized Poplar and Oak trees, I frequently welcomed its arrival. Today, I welcomed it with even greater appreciation, as my hope was *the Light* reaching within would help facilitate a shift in Gail's gloomy disposition.

After Gail had seated herself, I announced we would now discuss *how Humanity and their physical world came into existence.* This version, though, would contain factual variants, and fascinating twists and turns, compared to how the story was usually told. With Gail still not engaging, I decided I would try to help her overcome her woes.

Unsure how to proceed, I asked, "Gail, how can I help?"

"I don't know," she sighed, while biting her lip.

"Okay…" I considered my approach. "Are you still upset most people on Earth don't experience love as you did today?"

"Yes, but it's about something else now too. A thought that crossed my mind during our lunch discussion."

"And that is?" I prompted.

"Well…" she looked at me with tears in her eyes, "I'm unsure peace on Earth is achievable. Because," she shifted her gaze downward, "of who Humanity is. It's due to their nature, with their desire always rising and them always wanting *more*."

She then exhaled deeply, dropped her head into her hands, and mumbled to herself, "More wealth… more things… always wanting *more and most* of everything compared to anyone else."

"Oh…" I lingered, feeling confused and concerned. Wanting to understand, I gestured she continue.

"It's about their desire for *more* and how it currently expresses itself. For example, having more likes, followers, possessions, and fame takes precedence over having more peace on Earth. Sure, humans want to see peace happen. Yet, as you said when we first met, there's no plan in place to get themselves there. Peace simply isn't their priority."

"Right…" I nodded, now clearly understanding.

"This needs to change," her gaze met mine, "and the question is, how do we get Humanity focused on getting to peace? Rather than chasing the *mores* that are meaningless in how they exist."

"That's easy," I answered, knowing the solution. "We will share the Truths of their historic account with them. Then they can see the *big picture* too, and what kind of *more* needs to happen for them to achieve peace."

"But what if they don't listen to us? Or implement any kind of *Awakening Plan* to reach that place?" She bit her lip again.

"Gail," I leaned in, hoping to ease her concerns, "we are not going to approach this from a *'what-if'* perspective since that only focuses on problems, not solutions. We will bypass them also because, in a world where *free will* exists, and always will to my understanding, *what-ifs* are a waste of time."

With no comment from her, I continued.

"We are also not going to spend our time worrying about whether Humanity will accept their Truths or a plan for peace because that's equally ineffective. What we can do, though, is move forward with you receiving their Truths and the *Awakening Plan for Peace*. This, as we both know, increases their odds exponentially."

Gail paused, considering what I had proposed. I paused too, due to her increasing doubts, wondering if fear had approached. Was it aware of the progress we were making? Did it know we had returned to Earth? I had not sensed that was true, yet frequently fear silently lies in wait. I noted my concern with it now having access to us and decided to investigate later.

Shortly after our pause, her expression softened. "I'm sorry about my worries."

"Gail, you never need to apologize for how you awaken," I assured her. "Since fears and doubts are additional hurdles you'll help Humanity overcome."

"Okay…" she replied, and then she fell silent.

I quieted too, contemplating how to draw her back into our intended discussion. Fortunately, I remembered what had worked previously.

"Ready?" I asked.

"For what?" She looked up.

"For this…

"Once upon a time, in a not so far, far, far away land…" I exaggerated, with a giant sweep of my hand, "there was a collective of souls with their Omniscient in tow, who were seen headed Southbound to the place they'd call home."

Gail half-smiled, then took in a deep breath, followed with an expansive exhale. Feeling a possible shift in her mood, I sat quietly so as not to disturb her oncoming peace.

After several more breaths, Gail announced, "Your ploy has paid off… I'm ready to receive."

"Hooray!" I cheered.

"Okay, okay," she smiled, while playfully rolling her eyes, "now that you have successfully steered me from my worrisome ways, let's talk about how the creation of Humanity plays out.

"My first question is," she fully engaged, "does your version of their story vary significantly from how it's typically told? Because the way Humanity's souls first incepted, in the realm of Creation, has remained an unknown for most."

"That's a great question! And the answer is, there are similarities, yet it differs considerably."

"What's the primary point of differentiation?"

"Well…" I considered, "it can be found within *the whoms of who* inspired Humanity's existence."

"Oh… that's right. Because it was the Founders' desires and motivations that brought it about."

"You are correct. Yet," I importantly noted, "don't confuse that with *the whom of who* was the inspiration behind all that was initially created."

"All right then…" she grinned, showing her mood shift had come full-circle. "You've piqued my interest. Therefore, my questions are… What's the difference in comparison to how the story is usually told? How did you obtain this information? And just how did Humanity incept and commence?"

"That's a mouthful," I laughed, and then I thought about how to approach her numerous questions. When found, I said, "Okay, first, regarding 'how did I obtain this information?' The answer is, I visited the location where Humanity's creation event took place."

"You what?" Her eyes widened.

"It's true," I nodded.

"How did you accomplish that?"

"Well, without having to dive into a deep physics explanation, let's just say I dropped in and listened to their conversations. Also, I observed what occurred as it happened. Which was possible because past, present, and future only exist for those who are unawakened."

"Really, truly? You listened and watched as it all played out?"

"I did." I grinned ear to ear, for my incredible experience.

"Wow…" she relaxed into the sofa, "if that's the case, then I'm ready to hear and receive your account in how Humanity came to exist."

"Yay!" I thrilled, because I was more than ready to share how they commenced and incepted. To make sure I did not miss out on her readiness, I immediately launched Humanity's story by reading my findings to her.

"Okay, then…" I began, "we left off where the souls and their Omniscient were seen heading toward the new realm of Love. After arriving and settling in, the souls gathered together and encircled their Omniscient. They then called for a moment of silence to express their gratitude for all they were given. Not only for their new home and dimension but also for the remarkable *whom* they were gifted.

"After giving thanks," I continued, "their appreciations gave way to celebration! A festivity, of which, resounded throughout all of existence. This, of course," I smiled, looking up from my notes, "prompted thousands of souls from beyond, to migrate Southward to partake in the momentous occasion. All because they, too, desired to exist in a brand-new way.

"With nearly every realm now fully represented, everyone anxiously waited for what would happen next. In the interim, the souls mingled, chatted, bonded, and acquainted themselves. Soon after their meet and greet session, their Omniscient called for an audience. Eager to begin, all souls gathered for the incredible purpose of discussing the details in how Humanity would come into existence."

Pausing momentarily, I looked to Gail to see if she was following along. With her nod of yes, I continued.

"After everyone had settled in, the Omniscient welcomed them all and asked if they would like to begin. Of course, the souls answered with a thunderous, 'YES!' Their Omniscient laughed for their enthusiasm, then asked if there were any questions before proceeding. One soul stood and informed there were none. However, there was a message they needed to convey. The message was, they were beyond grateful their Omniscient had agreed to participate.

"First, because without that agreement, their venture into the vast unknown would have been impossible. Second, despite being given creative abilities, they knew they were incapable of creating a whole new life experience without assistance. With their message delivered, the room grew silent, and then all souls poured every ounce of love they had within them each onto their Omniscient. This, of course, resulted in… "

"Another giant love-fest!" Gail finished my sentence.

"Yes! Which then had everyone present, including their Omniscient, experiencing love yet again greater than ever before. That's because the souls now knew how outstanding it was to have their very own, forevermore, Divine. Also, because they realized the love and bond they shared with their Omniscient was the most precious gift they had ever been given."

"Wow…" Gail softly exhaled. Then she said, "How fortunate Humanity was to have their entire existence founded on that kind of love."

"I agree. And, Gail," I asked, "is this the same love you experienced beyond the veil today?"

"It is…" She closed her eyes, likely drifting to that place.

I drifted too… into the greatest love that has ever existed. This I did so I could experience the adoration Humanity collectively once had for their Omniscient. Also, so I could feel the affection they once had for one another, as even I have not felt love like that before anywhere in all of existence.

When I finished my experience, I opened my eyes to find Gail had completed hers. I then asked, "Do you have questions before we proceed?"

"No," she shook her head. "What I really want most now… is to hear *more*."

I laughed, considering her previous meltdown over that topic. Gail also laughed, sending a quirky smile my way, indicating she had realized the irony of her request too. With her desire for *more* understood, and wanting to proceed, I moved us forward.

"Okay, Gail, as said, the souls and their Omniscient were swept away into yet another love-fest. Shortly after, once everyone had recovered, their Omniscient asked what they would like their new experience to include. Excited to begin, the souls shouted out their too-numerous-to-count suggestions! In the chaos of it all, with it being difficult to hear their recommendations, the Omniscient called for a 'Time-out!' It was then recommended the souls select representatives, a Committee, to organize and account for everything they were requesting. Everyone agreed this was a brilliant idea! Because the *big picture* of what they desired most would show itself through the process.

"Now understand, and it's important to know," I glanced at Gail, "the Committee members, *eight in total*, were selected from amongst their peers versus being assigned by their Divine. They each had stellar credentials and previous leadership skills, which is why they each gained the souls' votes of confidence. And it was because of their qualifications it was decided they would serve evermore as Humanity's liaisons in all official matters."

"Excuse me," she interrupted, "are the Committee members the Founders by chance? The eight souls who originated realm traveling?"

"They are! Good catch." I gave her a thumbs-up, and then I continued.

"Upon their selection, the Committee set up shop to receive and log the soul's recommendations. Then, they suggested everyone pool their collective inventiveness and submit their summed intentions.

Interestingly," I noted, "it was during their creative process that the commencement of Humanity's soul families began evolving."

Gail tilted her head.

"This came about," I answered her unspoken question, "as souls gravitated toward one another and bonded over similar *how to exist goals*. Summed, souls founded their eternal relationships on what they individually desired and wanted most."

"Hmm… this makes sense," Gail bobbed her head. "Their most meaningful relationships were based on having like ideas in how to live."

"That's correct."

"What happened next?" she asked.

"After receiving all suggestions, the Committee organized and prioritized a list, then they submitted it to the Omniscient. After its reception, the Omniscient reviewed its entirety, then asked the souls to gather in. While they convened, still mingling and bonding, their Omniscient was suddenly overcome with profound adoration. It was then, in that very moment, with emotion still being a new experience for an Omniscient, their Divine vowed *'to love, care for, and do everything possible to always and endlessly please them.'* "

"Once the souls had settled in," I furthered their story, "their Omniscient welcomed them back. Then it was explained they'd now discuss what was of greatest importance to them. Specifically, by a majority, what they had agreed to found their existence on. With that noted, their Omniscient asked if anyone knew what their number one request was.

"Instantly, the souls shouted, 'LOVE!' Their Omniscient laughed for their enthusiasm, then confirmed love was their top priority. The souls collectively nodded it was true, as the newfound love they were experiencing was what they wanted most."

"What else was on the list?" Gail asked, looking fascinated.

"According to the Omniscient, in the order of importance, the remainder of their list was as follows… joy, peace, family, adventure, diversity, purpose, and longevity."

"They asked for 'diversity' specifically?" She looked confused.

"They did, in how they and everything would exist, since they knew they were predisposed to losing interest easily. Therefore, diversity was their solution."

"Then why does Humanity turn on one another due to their differences if they requested diversity?" Gail wrinkled her brow.

"I'll disclose that when we address your next question, *why does Humanity not live in peace?*"

"Okay," she nodded, so I continued.

"After the Omniscient had shared the list, a concerned looking soul quickly stood and said something significant was missing from it! Specifically, they wanted their Omniscient as the Divine to always partake in their experience. When all souls realized that request was mistakenly omitted, they asked it to be added to their list immediately. Their Omniscient smiled, then obliged, and thanked them for their thoughtful endearments.

"With priorities now established," I continued, "their Divine then asked if they were ready to start creating their new existence. This is when…"

"Wait!" Gail held up a hand, signaling alarm. "The souls helped with their own creation?"

I laughed because the souls had reacted the same way. I then answered her question by continuing the account of Humanity's inception.

"When the souls were asked, 'if they were ready to start creating their new existence,' everyone looked about the room in a state of confusion. Then, many expressed their great concern over the opportunity to take responsibility for their entire creation! The Omniscient reminded them, 'they were gifted the ability to accomplish all things.' This response created a panic, which sent the souls scurrying into a meeting to discuss the suggestion.

"When discussions were complete, the Committee approached to explain their collective opinion. They were grateful for the offer to assist with their creation, yet they decided it was best for the Omniscient to create its entirety. Summed, instead of the souls taking the lead, they asked for everything to be fabricated from their Divine's unlimited knowingness. That's because the Omniscient's inspirations would far exceed anything inspired by themselves only."

"With their desires understood, their Omniscient graciously agreed to orchestrate a remarkable experience for them. This, of which," I importantly noted, "was contingent on them each taking full responsibility to oversee the wellbeing of everything created. Summed, they were to care for all gifted to them *as an Omniscient would*. Of course, their Divine's request gained unanimous approval!"

"Um…" I heard Gail say, so I looked up. "They've not fulfilled that agreement."

"I know, they fell unconscious," was all I said, so we could continue enjoying the moment.

"With agreements complete," I chimed, to keep the mood upbeat, "their assigned Divine got straight to work. The plan was to create a remarkable place where the souls could live and exist. The intention was to abundantly fill it with everything they'd requested. Of course," I added, "*with love leading the way*. Their Divine then settled into the creative process, with the ultimate purpose of designing the most stunning display of love and beauty to be found anywhere within all of existence."

"What was created first?" Gail leaned in, engaging as I had hoped.

"A place to call home…" I replied, "which would serve more than one purpose. First, as a location to live. Then, as the Omniscient's *sacred significant other*… who would serve with the Divine to support all life existing upon her."

"Oh…" Gail softly gasped. "Mother Earth, right?"

"Yes," I answered. "She's the additional higher consciousness, who upon her creation, agreed to assist with Humanity's exceptional experience."

Grateful for her service, I looked outside the window and whispered, "May peace soon be yours, dear Sister."

Gail also turned, looking outside, and whispered the same in reverence for her. Then, she looked back at me and asked that I continue.

"After the souls had a location to live, the Omniscient created support systems on and beyond Planet Earth. These, in total, were created to sustain all that would physically exist. The most important was *the Sun*, which would serve two purposes. First, to assist with the order in how all life on Earth would function. Foremost, in representation and embodiment *of the Light* from beyond. With hopes," I added, "no one would ever forget who they were in Truth and in consciousness as *the Light* itself.

"After the Sun…" I continued, "water, land, and an earthly atmosphere were added. Now understand, Gail," I said, making sure I had her full attention, "from what I saw, the Omniscient immensely enjoyed creating this all. Yet, what the Omniscient delighted in most was animating *Divinity itself*. That is, creating physicalities to artistically convey its magnificence."

"Whoa…" Gail shivered and scooted to the edge of the sofa. "By creating Humanity, right?"

"No…" I swayed my head slowly, side-to-side.

"Then what?"

"All else existing prior to them."

"Well…" she motioned, eagerly.

"Flora, fauna, trees. Oceans, rivers, streams. Mountains, jungles, savannah, and the list goes on and on. Including… the endless hues of blue coloring the skies."

"Whoa, again…" She wiggled, smiling. "What about the stars, planets, and Humanity's Universe? Were they made then too?"

"No, the creation of those came later, when Humanity wanted to experience something new, yet again."

"Okay…" Gail lingered, thinking about it. "The Omniscient created everything else when their desire took rise again?"

"No, instead…" I paused, inhaling deeply with the immensity of this Truth, "other than the animal species, and the moon which came later, Humanity themselves created the remainder. Of course," I noted, "with the Omniscient's guidance and assistance."

"Holy-moly…" Gail closed her eyes, shaking her head while placing her hands alongside her temples.

Knowing she was processing Truth, I waited for her to resurface.

Many moments later, she dropped her hands to her lap and opened her eyes.

"Were the souls aware of how exceptional their experience was? Like having the opportunity to build out an entire Universe?" she asked.

"Yes," I assured her. "They were highly aware of the phenomenal arrangements taking place to fulfill their desires and dreams. Which had left them as you and I, enchanted and mesmerized beyond comprehension."

"I imagine so…" She slowly nodded, and then she asked, "So what happened after that?"

"Once the support systems were created and placed, the souls took front row seats to view the Omniscient's most artistic creations. An undertaking of which, as deemed by the souls, was their Omniscient's most playful and enjoyable sequence. Not only for their Divine, equally for them, since the creation of the remainder was the most fascinating and enchanting process to witness.

" 'How incredibly awesome our Omniscient is!' they marveled. 'Creating the most fantastic, unique, and unto us only species to ever exist.' Awestruck, the souls then whispered amongst themselves how loved they must be. After all, the diversity they'd requested now existed in endless multiplicities!

"After finishing the creation of it all, except Humanity themselves, the Omniscient asked if everything was to their liking. Everyone present replied it was beyond their wildest dreams! They also expressed how grateful they were their collective inception was not lessened by their limited perception. Embracing their confirmation and appreciations, their Omniscient shared what the intentions had been.

"First, it was to create a home containing all they had desired, requested, and wanted. Then, it was to fabricate everything needed for them and all species to coexist in harmony. Finally, the Omniscient had created wide-open spaces so they could equally express themselves artistically."

"I love this story!" Gail fidgeted, while clapping her hands.

Caught up in the moment, I clapped too, and then I continued.

"The Omniscient then talked about the spectacular species Humanity would reside with. Most importantly, the animal varieties and how they would partake in their experience. First, some existed for the simple purpose of their enjoyment. That is, all creatures great and small were created beautifully and uniquely to endlessly capture the soul's interests. Then, some were created for Humanity to have companionship. This, their Omniscient noted, they would not understand as a practice initially, yet in time they would.

"The souls nodded in understanding, then took a moment to observe everything created for them. When complete, they then declared, they would never get bored again! Everyone agreed, life on Earth was created to satisfy their adventuresome nature for eternities. With immense appreciation, they thanked their Omniscient for everything gifted to them."

"Excuse me, what about food?" Gail asked. "How did that work?"

"Are you asking if there was an additional purpose for the animal species?"

"Yes," she answered. "And other food resources too."

"Well, the Truth is, at the inception of Humanity's existence, food was not needed to physically exist. Eating to sustain life was not necessary until much later."

"They didn't need to eat?" She seemed surprised by the concept.

"They did not. Yet, some souls did eat the bounty produced from the plant species, namely the fruit."

Gail giggled and glanced at me sideways. "Were there any apples involved?"

I wagged my finger at her, gave her the don't go there look, and then continued their story.

"After the souls had expressed their appreciation, the Omniscient announced the time had come to create their physical existences. Intrigued, they asked how that would be accomplished. The Omniscient explained the materials that were used to create everything else would provide what was needed for them to take form. Additionally, the resources that initially brought them into existence at the Point of Inception would be incorporated. After all, it was important to have their first inception as *the Light* represented in their newly constructed compositions."

"What did their bodies look like?" Gail looked to me, with increasing curiosity. "Because I assume they were nothing like the ones humans have now."

"Correct, there's little resemblance."

"Okay, but what did they look like?" she asked again, impatiently.

"Oh…" I laughed, "you want details. Well, their earthly bodies were mostly ethereal, not overly tactile, and they had the graces their soul bodies did. Initially, Humanity took on an otherworldly appearance since they were filled with *the Light* from beyond. And take note," I highlighted, "these are the types of bodies Humanity will occupy again if they choose to awaken and transition into an era I call the *Paradigm of Peace*."

"Too cool!" Gail lit up with the prospect.

"I know!" I fully agreed.

"Next," I continued, "the Divine explained to the souls that their soon-to-be-created bodies would have an additional component integrated within them each. An addition of which, they would need to diligently use to mindfully fulfill their contracted agreements. Also, so that they could accomplish all they desired to achieve, in light of where they had recently located."

"Excuse me," Gail stopped me, 'mindfully?' "

"Yes, mindfully."

"I don't understand," she said, "it's the *mindful* thing that's confusing me. Can you please explain what *mindfully* means?"

"Sure, I'd be happy to."

I then let her know I would need to track down my notes to explain the details more thoroughly. With that, I set off to locate the white binder. While doing so, I took a moment to myself to accomplish some silent sleuthing. I decided to do this because Gail's earlier *what-if* worries had me questioning if fear had found us.

As I scanned everything in direct proximity, I saw no indication it had. So, I marked Gail's doubts up to her not having the same faith I had in Humanity's ability to awaken. Not wanting to draw fear's attention to us, or to the fact the *Awakening Plan* was successfully delivering, I quickly ended my search.

Chapter 20

Mindfulness, Mindfully, Minds

After retrieving the white binder, I asked Gail for a moment to myself so that I could review all facts needed to further her clarity. With her agreement, I turned to the section tabbed *Truth* and quickly scanned my notes regarding the topics of *Minds, Mindfully,* and *the First Intention Humanity set*. When I was clear on how to proceed, I let her know we could continue our discussion.

"Okay, Gail," I began, "we left off where the Omniscient just announced it was time to create the soul's earthly physicalities. The Omniscient then explained a new feature would be added to complete their experience. An addition they would need to use to satisfy all they desired to achieve within their newly created experience. And the means and way for them to accomplish it all…" I deliberately lingered.

"Get on with it!" she laughed.

"…was by using their very own… created by their Divine… *Minds*!" I excited with loving this Truth.

"So what?" Gail shrugged, "They have minds, that's nothing new."

"Seriously…" I stammered, surprised by her reply. "So what?"

"Yes," she nodded, and then shrugged her shoulders again.

"It's an amazing what!" I laughed, not letting her ambivalence deflate my excitement. "Because the *minds* the Omniscient gave to Humanity were unique, exceptional gifts. Unique, because other than an Omniscient, they were the only souls to have *minds*. Exceptional, because after they received them, Humanity possessed a consciousness of themselves only."

"Okay…" Gail blinked several times. "If I understand you correctly, your point is, no one in all of existence, except an Omniscient, had *minds* previously?"

"That's correct."

"That makes no sense," she scrunched her nose, "because minds should be standard equipment given to all conscious beings."

"Well…" I smiled, "they're not. In fact, from what I've seen and gleaned, individual *minds* are anomalies beyond this location."

"Then why would Humanity need them?"

"They'd need them primarily for the reasons the Omniscient stated," I replied. "First, so they could fulfill their contracted agreements. Also, so they could accomplish what they desired to achieve."

"Okay…" Gail squinted, "I'm still not making the connection as to why *minds* are so important. I think because none of this is relatable to what you've shared so far."

"Not true, dear Gail," I wiggled my eyebrows, "as aside from what the Omniscient conveyed, your clarity can also be found within the verbiage of Humanity's First Intention. This we discussed when you and I first met. Know though," I reassured her, "I don't expect you to recall that easily. Why do you think I keep this at hand wherever I am?" I held up the white binder, laughing.

"Because there's a whole lot of Truth to remember!" She laughed too. Then she asked me to refresh her memory on the First Intention's wording.

"Their First Intention was *to exist in yet another way*. Their aim was *to establish an additional, unique life experience exclusive to themselves.* Also, as we know, they asked for abilities to create in likeness to an Omniscient."

"Hmm…" Gail pressed her lips together, "let's see if I can figure this out."

She then drifted in thought, while I sat quietly watching the cogs of her consciousness spin. After several minutes, once her calculations were complete, she resurfaced.

"Okay, I think I understand why Humanity needed *minds*. First, it was so they could *actually*," she emphasized, "fulfill the agreements they contracted with their Omniscient. Which was to see to the wellbeing of everything created for them, *as an Omniscient would*. An undertaking, of which, would most likely require a *mind*.

"Another reason they would need *minds*," she continued, "was so they could *create in likeness to an Omniscient*, since without *minds*, that prospect would most likely be an impossibility. And..." she patted herself on the back, "I figured that one out all by myself, with you restating their First Intention."

"Correct you are!" I cheered.

Gail's eyes smiled. "It took a minute, but I finally got there. Did I list all the reasons why they would need *minds*? Or are there others?"

"There are two others of importance. First, so they could easily connect with the One Divine Mind and its consciousness. The other has to do with the Omniscient's *in light of where they had recently located* reference."

"And that is?"

"They would need *minds* because they'd requested to live autonomously, *unto themselves only*. Therefore, *minds* were necessary so that they could remain conscious and maintain consciousness while living in sequestered isolation. Does that make sense?"

"Not entirely..." she shook her head. "However, if you answer my initial question, 'what does mindfully mean,' then maybe I'll understand more easily."

"Right..." I laughed, and then I finally answered her question.

"Mindfully means... *to consciously do so*."

"Hmm..." Gail quietly hummed, "*mindfully means consciously*."

"It does. And," I continued, with her now tracking well, "for Humanity to *consciously* achieve all they desired most, they would need *conscious minds* to do so. Ultimately, because they were no longer living in direct proximity to the One Divine Mind. Which just happens to be the operating consciousness, *and eternal mindset,* for all who exist beyond Humanity's realm."

With that explained, I pulled an illustration from the white binder, and then went and sat next to Gail. Holding it before us both, I said, "This should bring the additional clarity you need."

THE ONE DIVINE MIND

The One Divine Mind is the consciousness of the Omnipotent Divine, and it is the operating consciousness for all existing beyond Humanity's experience: all realms, dimensions, beings, and souls.

POINT OF ORIGIN

POINT OF INCEPTION   POINT OF INCEPTION

LIGHT   LIGHT

CREATION   CREATION

TRUTH   TRUTH

UNCONDITIONAL   LOVE

ANGELIC   ANGELIC

CELESTIAL   CELESTIAL

UNIVERSAL   UNIVERSAL

TERTIARY   TERTIARY

PLANETARY   PLANETARY

Humanity's Existence is Lived Here

With Humanity living in separation from the One Divine Mind, they would now need a means and way to have consciousness. Therefore, they were gifted their very own *minds*.

(Dear Reader: visit www.MyCallingMyQuest.com to download a more readable illustration in a free PDF format. This includes all handouts within this book.)

"Oh…" Gail lingered, while studying the handout. "I understand the overall significance now. When Humanity was created, the souls were not given minds as we know them on Earth. Instead, they were given *minds* which we call *consciousness*."

"Exactly. Due to their desire to live independently, far from all existing beyond their realm, they were given *minds*. *Minds* that were teeming with the consciousness of the Omnipotent Divine."

"Wow…" she uttered, while continuing to view the handout.

"Are you ready for another 'Wow?' " I asked.

She looked to me, slowly nodding her yes.

"Not only were they gifted *minds* possessing the Omnipotents' consciousness, but they were also granted…" I paused, for optimum effect, "a portion of the Omniscients' abilities."

"What?" Her mouth dropped open. "The Omniscient Divines?"

"Yes," I nodded. "Humanity was given powerful abilities *in likeness to the Omniscients,* so they could achieve everything set forth within their First Intention."

"Powerful abilities…" Gail whispered, "like *Superpowers*?"

"Yes, like '*Superpowers*,' " I also whispered, pretending it was a secret only she and I knew.

"Though," I noted, "they were only given *measured degrees* of the Divine's abilities. Otherwise, they would have never survived the implementation of them."

"What powers were they given?" Gail turned herself sideways, facing me.

"*Mindfulness, Wisdom, Imagination, Demonstration, Discernment, Understanding,* and *Authority,*" I answered.

"Authority?"

"Yes, Authority. The sacred privilege to have dominion over their earthly experience."

"Seriously? They were given dominion?"

"Yes. It was sanctioned so they could effectively fulfill their promised agreements. Understand, though, dominion means *to tend to and care for*, not to rule or exercise power over another."

"I know, that's why I asked, because they're not using that power as it was designated."

I nodded, yet offered no comment.

"And I'm curious…" she moved us forward by posing her next question, "why were Love, Understanding, and Compassion not added to the powers gifted to Humanity? Because those are important too."

"That's an excellent question. It's because there was no need for understanding or compassion before Humanity descended in consciousness. That's because their only experience to this juncture was love, which exemplifies understanding and compassion."

"That makes sense," she nodded.

"Perfect," I said, while returning to my chair across the room. When I looked back at Gail, she had drifted elsewhere.

"Where are you?"

"I'm here..." she hesitated, then looked at me. "I'm just taken with everything you've shared... and amazed by how outstanding Humanity's account is. The boundless love, the endless opportunities, a realm of their own, and the abilities of an Omniscient."

I nodded, as Humanity's experience was incomparable.

"The other thought I had," she continued, "was that the *minds* Humanity incepted with are not the minds they currently use on Earth."

"You are correct, they are not. Instead, Humanity collectively uses their mortal minds. These provide them with the intelligence they need to see to their wellbeing with how they currently exist in consciousness. After all," I added, "they no longer possess the consciousness they were given."

"Oh, no..." she frowned, "is consciousness as it was a lost cause for Humanity?"

"No, it's not a lost cause," I answered, hoping she would not drop back into her worries. "Because the Omnipotent's consciousness is still available to everyone here if they choose to use it."

"Okay," Gail's brows lifted, "so everyone still has access to *it* as a resource?"

"Absolutely, everyone does... through connecting with the Omnipotent and aligning themselves with the One Divine Mind as *its* consciousness.

"And rest assured, Gail," I added, continuing to ease her concerns, "Humanity can live fully conscious on Earth again. It's all possible. All they must do is remedy what they eventually created and then they can collectively awaken. And as you know," I reminded her, "getting them to that place is why you and I have come together."

"I know. I'm silly sometimes… not so *mindfully* getting lost, worried, and distracted."

"It's easy to do here with fear ruling," I confirmed. Then I asked if she had any further questions.

"Not regarding this, but I have another. Can you please share the remainder of Humanity's story? Then, we can deliver their Truths sooner than later." She smiled, mindfully moving us forward to reach that goal.

"I'd love to!" I happily agreed. "Would you like to sum up where we are?"

"Yes," she nodded.

"We left off where…" she pondered, finding her way, "the souls were delivering appreciations for everything created and gifted to them. After that, their Omniscient announced it was time to create their physical existences, including a new addition.

"The addition?" Gail looked to me confidently. "*Minds.* They were given these for three important reasons. First, so they could see to the wellbeing of all gifted to them. Next, so they could fulfill all they desired to achieve. Finally, to make sure they remained conscious while living far from consciousness itself."

Gail paused, assessing if she had summed it all, and then announced, "That's all."

"Well done!"

Gail chuckled, grinned broadly, and asked, "What happened next?"

"Well…" I considered what to share. When found, I continued.

"After the souls were clear on the reasons you listed, their Omniscient disclosed the final reason *minds* were needed for their experience. The purpose was so they could equally care for themselves in physicality. After all, embodying the influence of an Omniscient was by far the most sacred allowance any soul had ever been given. In fact," I said, driving the point home, "the consciousness Humanity would soon possess was non-existent except to an Omniscient's experience.

"Once their responsibilities were restated," I continued, "their Omniscient asked one final time if they promised to adhere to their contracted agreements. With their excitement now cresting beyond containment, the founding souls of Humanity boomed their 'YES!' They then promised, assured, and vowed to mindfully, attentively, and responsibly meet every condition set forth.

"With that established, and their commitment secured, the souls encircled their Omniscient and anxiously awaited the next announcement. Knowing what the souls wanted most, their Omniscient then declared, 'Without further ado… I'll now create you!' "

"Yay!" Gail flung her arms into the air. "That's a chills moment!" Then she asked, "Did Humanity initially care for everything as promised?"

"Yes," I answered. "They took wonderful care of it all. Also, they diligently practiced *mindfulness,* as requested. All was in balance and in wonderful order as they learned to exist to their fullest potential."

"Good to hear…" Gail nodded. "What happened after that?"

"Once their physicalities were created, Humanity made their way to Planet Earth. When they arrived, they acquainted themselves with the wonders of their world. What did they love most? With the knowings they now had?"

Gail eagerly nodded, wanting to know.

"The Omniscient, Omnipotent Divines in total… equally, every amazing aspect They each contributed for Humanity's experience to unfold. As without Them all, not one single nanoparticle of their exceptional existence would have been available to them. Inclusive of, yet not limited to…" I trailed off, dropping into a cadence to conclude Acts One, Two, and Three.

"An inbound inauguration from the Point of Origin, where nothing yet exists. Rapidly burning through the highest ethers, as an essence of All that IS. The Point of Inception, heeding-receiving-providing all needed to exist as the Light itself. Beings of Light, come into existence, taking form as consciousness. Self-directing, self-sufficient, having life experiences. Thinking, speaking, intermingling through the harmonic tones.

"The realm of Creation, the Omniscient Divines, a multi-realm Universe. The making of souls, the choosing of homes, life with family and friends. Wanting something new, never had before, souls taking rise and traveling the realms. Ascending-descending, mastering consciousness, vowing allegiance to always seek more.

"Meeting and planning, soliciting Omniscients, requesting a brand-new existence. Graciously granted, lovingly gifted, a new realm is kindly created. An autonomous existence, a personal Omniscient, a loving Mother named Planet Earth. Species in multiplicities, ethereal

*physicalities, minds-powers-consciousness. And, last, but not least…
bestowed and bequeathed, were measures of Omnipotence.*

"Summed, dear Gail," I stood, took a seat on the floor, which prompted her to join me, "I have now delivered and you have received the full account in how all beings incepted. Inclusive of, yet not limited to, how Humanity themselves came into existence."

"Wow…" was all she said, while closing her eyes, as her body swayed with Truth.

Realizing she needed a moment, I quietly held space for her. Eventually, she resurfaced and opened her eyes.

"You know, I'm quite familiar with the creation story and how it's told on Earth. Yet, it's this version that's emotionally consumed me unlike any other. Because of…" she locked her eyes with mine, "*You.* Your eloquence, effectiveness, and infinite endearments for every element Humanity's story speaks to."

"No…" I shook my head adamantly, unwilling to accept credit for Truth's abilities. "You feel this way because this rendition is fully intact. Meaning, it's not missing facts that were forgotten or withheld."

"I disagree…" she whispered.

Then, unable to contain her appreciation any longer, Gail decanted her love and gratitude upon me. Already overwhelmed with the success of our collaborative quest, I surrendered and graciously received all she was giving. We lingered in that place for many moments, and then Gail looked to me and asked, "Shall we?"

Knowing what it was for, I smiled and answered, "Yes."

With my agreement, we both closed our eyes and searched for the place where Humanity had incepted. When found, we gleaned and gathered together the most remarkable love to have ever been known. Gail and I then wrapped that flood of love around Humanity's entire existence, hoping they would soon experience the splendor and opulence of it. As if they did, it would feel like a tidal wave of adoration… without a single condition or expectation found within it.

With synchronized, intentional breathing, Gail and I continued pouring that love upon them. That is, until we reached the place where our physicalities could no longer serve as conduits for it. Then, with our bodies taxed, abilities spent, and intentions complete, we acclimated ourselves to the conditions existing on Earth. When satisfied, we opened our eyes and scooted ourselves closer together.

Taking Gail's hands into mine, I then lavished her with my appreciation. I thanked her repeatedly for calling me out, and for tending to my failing hope. I praised her additionally for her formidable determination, which entirely established our remarkable collaboration. I then reminded her she was my *Angel of saving grace…* and Humanity's too, for relentlessly pursuing the Truths they needed to awaken.

After adorning her with my admirations, I leaned myself far into her comforting presence. Gail kindly received me with a warm embrace, and I rested in that place for countless minutes. Not only for the love we shared, but also for her reverence since I rarely encounter someone who shares the same passion to serve as me. When I had finished my experience, I released our embrace and asked if there was anything she needed before parting ways.

"No… I think it's time for us to stop for the day," she warmly smiled, "because I need time to process the Truths you conveyed."

She then asked me if we could please meet in three weeks, so she could *mindfully* review the entirety of how Humanity came into existence. I informed her that timing worked well for me because I needed to prepare for the topic we would discuss next: *Why is Humanity not living in peace?* With arrangements made, we both stood, embraced one final time, and then my dearest Gail set out on her way.

"Until soon…" I bid my farewell, with tears cascading down my cheeks. Tears filled with joy, hope, and relief, for her devotion and reception of the Truths contained within the *Awakening Plan for Peace.*

Later that evening, after resting, I gave great thanks that Humanity's incepting Truths had finally landed. The Truths the Mortal Majority had once deemed would successfully 'pave the way' to the fulfillment of their Third Intention. Happy for Humanity, fortunate for Gail and me, I extended appreciation for the ease of our journey to now.

Anticipating the day when we would meet again, I retrieved the piles of content I had commiserated with before Gail's second intervention. Surrounding myself with them as I previously had, I reveled in the fact that they had not accumulated in vain. Looking forward to sharing the 'what happened next' with her, I started reading the *Clarity* she had requested to advance Humanity's Awakening.

Midway through my read and review, I drifted off wondering if she was aware of how life on Earth was initially experienced. The eons of non-time before Humanity veiled, when everyone existed as *One* in peace, joy, and harmony. Did she know Humanity and their Omniscient once resided on Earth together? That the souls had mastered the use of their minds, consciousness, and powers? It was a remarkable time in Humanity's history… as they, with their Divine, created awesome newness alongside one another.

Then, while basking in the bliss of their exceptional experience, I caught sight of the fallout from their Second Intention. Humanity's conscious descent, the demise of it all, and the outcomes resulting from every choice they made and story they told. Unwilling to approach those Truths quite yet, I quickly opened my eyes and ended my daydream. I gathered the content I had surrounded myself with and then returned it to the room from where I had retrieved it.

While doing so, I told myself, "That can wait…" since I would not allow those Truths to dampen my joy. The Truths that had shattered my heart into thousands of pieces, the ones that had rendered me useless the moment I found them.

"Yes, I'll save those for another day…" I heard myself say, since the time was now for a well-deserved break.

Afterword

And that, dear Humanity, is how you came to exist… according to what I have gleaned, tracked, and mapped. Please know, even though I assert all I have shared is real and true, I highly encourage you to question every fact and Truth. Quiet yourself, expand your awareness, and practice seeking Truth for yourself. Choose to awaken, put your rising consciousness to the test, and you, too, will discover how exceptional your experience is.

Is there more to discover beyond what I have shared? Absolutely! I only retrieved the essentials. I did not turn every stone, hoping you would launch your own quest for Truth. Though, for you to reach the places Gail and I have, you must first awaken. Additionally, if you want to achieve harmony and wellbeing for yourselves and all gifted to you, you must awaken. Fortunately, you are well on your way through receiving your highest Truths.

If you choose to ascend in consciousness with the *Awakening Plan for Peace*, you additionally will need the *Clarity* and *Hope* Gail came to retrieve. *Clarity* about your experience on Earth after your creation, how you lost the consciousness you were given, and why peace for all existing in your world continually eludes you. *Hope* through thorough instruction in how you and Humanity can awaken, and a review of the moral code you established that prevents a global reconciliation. Yes, all of that and even more is yet to come, when the remainder of *My Calling, My Quest* publishes.

With that explained, I would like to address a couple of items before we part ways. Let's begin with fear to further your understanding of how I am referring to it. First, there is fear as a psychological, emotional, and physical experience, which impacts nearly every species existing on Earth. I will forgo an explanation of this type of fear because your understanding of the premise is universal. The fear I will speak to, though, is *fear as a Foe,* which I have named *fear itself.*

Itself? Yes, *itself.*

Does this indicate *fear* is a whom? It does not; instead, it is only a what. Though true, do not assume that diminishes the fact that *fear itself* has the capacity to establish and accomplish its own agenda. We will cover this in detail when we meet again, yet I will share a brief description of what *fear* is to establish the basis.

Summed, *fear itself* is an entity, though it is not an actual being. Nevertheless, it does possess the ability to assess its environment and input its findings for the benefit of achieving its own mission and goals. It also possesses intelligence, the ability to acquire and apply knowledge and skills. It has a consciousness as well; therefore, it is aware of its existence. Additionally, *fear itself is a consciousness,* the ruling consciousness on Planet Earth. It currently serves as Humanity's collective consciousness, and it is now the consciousness from which all life on Earth must live and function. And, as reported previously, it is Humanity who created it.

"Whoa…" as Gail would say, right?

Agreed, since the complexities of what *fear itself* is, as an agent with intelligence, was even shocking for me. Interestingly, people on Earth still believe the achievement of advanced artificial intelligence, *the theory of mind and self-awareness*, still eludes them. However, when fear was created, Humanity reached that benchmark nearly immediately. And that is all I will share for now, as when we meet again, the topic of fear will be at the forefront of Gail's and my discussions.

Speaking of Gail and fear, even though she and I have fared well so far, the remainder of our journey was less favorable. In the end, fear did gain awareness of our progress after we returned from the realm of Truth. And, when it did, it took aim to destroy my mission again through plotting, scheming, and organizing itself to maintain its rule on Earth.

Fortunately, Gail and I survived the ordeal, yet it was not without trials and tribulations. In fact, after Gail and I parted ways in November of 2017, it has taken me three years to deliver these Truths to you. Of course, a portion of that time was due to publishing needs, yet the remainder was due to conflicts with fear. How did I finally reach this place despite fear's disruptions? How have I managed its endless attempts to end my quest? I utilized every recommendation contained within the *Awakening Plan for Peace*.

The great news is, if I overcame fear's onslaughts to keep Truth from delivering, you have an excellent chance to awaken with the same means and way. How do I know this if I am already awake? I know it because Gail and others have successfully advanced their conscious ascensions with the *Awakening Plan*. Additionally, they have visited distant realms to assist with Humanity's Awakening here, *There*, and beyond, just like me.

It's true, and hopefully, some of them will step forward and bravely share their experience as I have shared mine with you. And just so you know, as not to confuse, when we travel to the beyond, it is through our conscious abilities. That means our earthly bodies remain on Planet Earth.

The next item I would like to address concerns a question I am frequently asked. The question is, "what can I do now" to facilitate peace until *Clarity* and *Hope* deliver? My suggestion is you set an intention to wake up from your unconscious predicament if you have not already.

In other words, *commence your Awakening* and commit to the advancement of constructive change for all existing on Earth. Once committed, initiate a plan of action with the ability to facilitate your Awakening for the advancement of peace. I know it sounds like a huge undertaking, yet I promise impactful progress is possible through taking small steps. Steps that are reasonable and not overly time-consuming. The steps I recommend you begin with are as follows.

First, I suggest you put the *Daily Practice for Peace* to use. This is the practice that founded the *Awakening Plan*, which contains the five principles others have used to ascend in consciousness. They are also the five principles I utilize to maintain my consciousness while serving amidst the chaos and conditions existing on Earth. As mentioned before, the principles are:

Start Being the Change, Today
Choose Your Stories Wisely
Love More than You Fear
Create Consciously and Responsibly
Seek the Best and Highest for All

We will cover these extensively when we meet again, yet until then, I would like to highlight a couple of items. First, take note of the words *Start* and *Today* in the first *Daily Practice for Peace*, as their importance is significant. Significant, because, if you truly want to help advance peace, *you must be the first person* (every single day of the week) *to start expediting the change you desire to see.* You must also be the first to demonstrate the changes *you believe* are mandatory for peace to suffice.

Follow that with *choosing your stories wisely* and mindfully monitoring your every word so as not to cause harm to others. If you are unable to choose them effectively, then please say nothing at all. The critical verbiage human beings use to demean one another must stop because it impedes your capacity to collectively awaken. There is a lot to lose if you choose otherwise, so please quit criticizing and tearing down one another. And, if you are not the one issuing the condemnations, then stop allowing others to pummel you with their hate and destruction.

Correspondingly, I recommend you change the way you manage your social media accounts, or consider forgoing them entirely. I know these are not popular recommendations. However, at the very least, I ask you to please consider *turning off* the comments section. Shut down the hate, assist with lessening the levels of conscious pollution, and take responsibility for your and Humanity's wellbeing. Initially, you may miss the attention, praises, and the boosting of ego; yet in Truth, those too hinder your collective Awakening.

Finally, I recommend combining the following five practices with the *Daily Practice for Peace*. The first four are known as *The Four Agreements* by don Miguel Ruiz. They are quite simple, yet they are powerful and embody the ability to facilitate incredible change. As well, they have advanced your collective Awakening on Earth to immense degrees already.

The fifth practice listed, which delivered to Humanity thousands of years ago, is the most imperative for peace to prevail. Its importance was qualified and thoroughly conveyed, yet nearly everyone on Earth refuses to put their judgments to rest… even though *not judging others* would restore peace rather quickly. In fact, if humans continue refusing to relinquish their judging ways, Humanity will never reach peace.

The additional five practices are:

Be Impeccable with Your Word
Don't Take Anything Personally
Don't Make Assumptions
Always Do Your Best
Judge No One, Practice Accountability Instead

In closing, for those who believe I am just telling another version of *the same old story* to sway your beliefs, then I highly recommend you *wake up* and launch your own Truth-Seeking mission. Begin your adventure into the vast unknown, question every Truth I have shared, and then seek to prove me wrong or seek to prove me right, as either way, you will discover *it is insignificant* upon your Awakening. Insignificant, because, at the root of Humanity's conflicting theories and belief debates, it is not an *either/or* dilemma. In fact, theist wisdoms are not the only place where you will discover Truth, since Truth is well-founded throughout many scientific and agnostic teachings.

For instance, the belief that "the Omniscient is vital and essential" for humans to exist, is equally true to "the Omniscient is irrelevant and unnecessary." Unnecessary? Yes, because that is the precedent you set when you veiled yourselves and severed ties with the Divine. Irrelevant? Yes, because when you as Humanity set out to fully express yourselves as creative beings, *your relevance and significance* were what you prioritized and endorsed primarily. Evolution is factual too, equal to creation, because after you lost consciousness and the light rescinded from within, evolution was necessary for you to survive the conditions you collectively created.

Yes, those each, and thousands of similar contradictions, are verifiable Truths if you awaken.

In closing, there are three final items I would like to mention.

First, if your current beliefs have you struggling with the fact that there is more than one Omniscient, I kindly refer you to Genesis 1:26.

Second, please remember that *you are so much more than just a human*. It seems like everywhere I turn, I hear, "I'm only human" and similar phrases. I mention this because these beliefs and colloquialisms greatly hinder your and Humanity's growth. They limit your conscious advancement and entirely flatten your learning curve.

Finally, please be kind to one another… *love more than you fear*. Extend compassion and understanding to all whom you encounter, as everyone on Earth is trying to survive the conscious conditions existing here. *Seek the best and highest for all* as well, as it is the only way to ensure the viability of all species on Earth. You can achieve this by thoroughly evaluating every choice and decision you make.

With that all said, and until we meet again, I thank you for your thoughtful consideration of the Truths I share and deliver.

With appreciation,

C.W. Isaac

Addendum

Hello and welcome!

If you have arrived here before your read, then you have decided an introduction and guidance on how to proceed would benefit your Awakening experience. I understand this because, before *My Calling, My Quest* published, some readers expressed they felt lost and confused without an introduction. If you are arriving here after completing your read, then I encourage you to continue since I will cover topics others conveyed were of importance. For instance: what type of book this is, its target audience, its intention and purpose, and how to use it for optimum effect.

Let's begin with *My Calling, My Quest* not resembling most books you have read. Specifically, its genre, since I have never quite figured out how to classify it. It is a book helping one transform with a story, yet it ventures from the boundaries of transformational fiction. It also strays from a non-fiction, self-help format, yet it may serve as one of the most life-changing books you will ever read. If it is neither of these, yet it is transformative in its abilities, then what is it?

I have named and classified it as *non-fiction, transformation through story conveyance*. Was self-classifying an easy way out, excusing me from meeting literary standards of excellence? Absolutely not. Instead, it had to do with priorities and transparency. I chose to prioritize your opportunity to awaken over hiding behind an ambiguous or fictional genre. In other words, I am fully disclosing *My Calling, My Quest* is a true story to ensure the advancement of Humanity's Awakening.

Understand, choosing to disclose my Truth, my purpose, and my unique state of consciousness requires incredible courage. Though true, executing transparency is an easy choice to make. Easy, because for you as Humanity to awaken, it is imperative you know who you are in Truth. Additionally, for you to accomplish peace, it is essential you understand what you are exclusively capable of. If you are unaware of what to aim for, then you will never achieve your highest potential. Nor will you ever develop the ability to reach the conscious destinations I and others have.

I would consider this an epic fail.

Next, let's discuss who I wrote *My Calling, My Quest* for and who is its target audience. First and foremost, I wrote it for the entirety of Humanity. I know, on Earth, the experts say claiming everyone as your audience is presumptuous and unwise. However, considering the predicament Humanity finds itself in, and *My Calling, My Quest* providing a way to awaken, I would say my choice is forgivable. I would also say it is allowable since delivering a means and a way to peace is what Humanity commissioned me to achieve.

Aside from penning *My Calling, My Quest* for all of Humanity, I wrote it for every individual who is ready to advance their Awakening. Fortunately, living in peace individually is entirely possible until Humanity accomplishes the same. How do I know this? I know it because when you as Humanity were created, you were given incredible abilities to accomplish all things, including achieving peace. This you will discover within.

With an understanding of who I wrote *My Calling, My Quest* for, I would like to share this book's intention. From the beginning, the intention of *My Calling, My Quest* was singular and simple: deliver a way to awaken for Humanity's achievement of peace. Though that was the sole aim, other intentions began satisfying themselves along the way. First, Gail's intention to ascend in consciousness furthered exponentially. (*You will meet Gail soon.*) Second, my intention to fulfill my mission on Earth is finally succeeding. Take note, both outlying intentions progressed by engaging with the Truths presented within. Therefore, as disclosed when opening this book, only proceed when you are fully prepared to embrace Truth's transformative abilities.

Finally, with that all conveyed, let's discuss how you can best utilize *My Calling, My Quest*. I offer this because people have asked, "What am I supposed to do with this book?" The answer is, you need not do anything with it initially, except sit back, relax, and receive. Enjoy the incredible insights, discover Humanity's astounding potential, and lean into all the possibilities unfolding before you. And, please understand, the purpose of *My Calling, My Quest* is not for you to dive in and fully comprehend every concept immediately. Instead, its purpose is for you to receive your phenomenal, beyond imaginable Truths.

After finishing your read and allowing yourself time to assimilate, I would then consider using *My Calling, My Quest* for a new purpose; for instance, as an educational resource from which to learn and study. If waking to reach peace is truly your intent, then you and Humanity will need to improve your understandings. Additionally, you will need to expand your perspectives. Otherwise, your situation on Earth will never resolve. Fortunately, improvement, expansion, and resolution are at hand through studying the historic Truths *My Calling, My Quest* presents.

For your convenience, you can visit www.MyCallingMyQuest.com to download and print a free PDF copy of this manuscript. Once you have printed the PDF text, you can then highlight, mark it up, and organize Humanity's Truths for how you learn best. This workbook copy is available at no cost through the contributions of BePeaceOnEarth.org. This is the nonprofit organization I and others founded to ensure everyone has access to the sum of their Truths.

During your study, consider keeping a list of your questions. Upon completing your read, if they are still unanswered, visit the website listed above and submit them to us via the Contact Us page. Once we have received them, we will develop additional resources to assist with your learning curve needs.

In closing, as stated previously, I cannot begin to express how thrilled I am *My Calling, My Quest* has made its way to you. Reaching this place was quite the feat, yet thankfully, it was achievable through the *Truth, Clarity,* and *Hope* I deliver. That said, and with you receiving all needed to proceed, you can now direct yourself back to the beginning. I ask you to please commence your read with the Author's Note, as it provides the basis for *My Calling, My Quest's* entire purpose.

Wishing you a wonderful read and a happy commencing your Awakening day!

Acknowledgments

It took a village and some miracles, too, for *My Calling, My Quest* to publish. The following are those I want to thank, as their contributions were essential for its completion.

First and foremost, Appio Claudius Hunter, as without him, *My Calling, My Quest* would not have published. He is the incredible human being who stepped up to the plate and bravely put on the super-hero cape to ensure Humanity receives all needed to awaken. His courageous, momentous, collaborative agreement now ensures all people on Earth have access to their Truths. He has mindfully and tirelessly pursued his own conscious ascension so that he can effectively help Humanity achieve an Awakening. Thank you, dear Appio, for your love of Humanity, and for your tireless dedication to see to their wellbeing: I see you, I honor you, and I cherish you, always and evermore.

My mom and dad, Karen and Cliff, for their agreement to facilitate my physical existence. Also, for their perfected upbringing of me, which allowed me to remain unveiled. Additionally, my stepparents Ron and Toni, for their contributions and assistance with parenting me amidst my unique challenges. I extend that same love and appreciation to my beautiful siblings, nieces, nephew, grandparents, aunts, uncles, cousins, and to Evie—another mother in proxy when needed. We made it, we survived it, I love you all dearly!

Eshwa for his endless love and devotion, Annette for her care and efforts to support us, Dylan for the depth of our shared understandings, Brittny for her insights and inspiration, Curtis for our new, incredible heartfelt connection, Aunt Janet and Tara for their faith in my mission, Mary for her constructive, entertaining Truth assimilation, Mark for our phenomenal otherworldly discussions, Mindy for helping me overcome fear when I needed it most, Jim for our heart and soul adorations, Christiana for her unrivaled curiosity and affection, Ronalafae for her authenticity and love of Humanity, my bestie Rachel for her support and patience no matter the circumstance, don Jose for helping me when my rising consciousness nearly swept me away, and Mike for introducing me to some of the most incredible human beings I have encountered on Earth. And, a special shout out to Kierra, Kahlianna, Emily, Mamadou, Stacey, Tasha, Regena, Grant, Dusty, Kevin, Laura, Jodie, and Livvie for their love, support, and contributions.

The professionals who assisted with publishing, manuscript assessment, and editing: Carrie Jareed, Tara Manriquez, Dorit Sasson, Corinne Dixon, Appio Hunter, Micah (MJ) Schwader, and Christine Kloser, who coached me in 2015 to establish a solid foundation from where I could launch my highest calling and quest.

Finally, and most importantly, Humanity's magnificent Omniscient Divine, as my calling and quest would have failed without your love, wisdom, and guidance. My devotion to you and yours is eternal, and I am honored to serve and assist with reestablishing peace throughout your realm. My gratitude, of course, extends to the incredible Omniscient Divines entirely, for overseeing my wellbeing every step of the way. Your perspectives are crucial to our mission's success and your advisements, as said, are priceless.

Again, I thank you each, I love and adore you immensely.

C.W. Isaac

Glossary

All of Existence
Everything existing beneath the Point of Origin, including Humanity's realm.

All that Exists
All existing beneath the realm of Creation, excluding Humanity's realm.

(The) **All that IS**
aka: The Omnipotent Divine
It is the Light.
It is what affords us each the opportunity to exist.
It is the highest source of support we can utilize to sustain our wellbeing.

Ascend in Consciousness
The progression of our awareness, for the benefit of living awakened.

Awakening Plan for Peace
A means and way to achieve peace on Earth, which provides the Truth, Clarity, and Hope Humanity requested to advance their Awakening.

(The) Beyond

All realms and locations outside of Humanity's experience.

(The) Committee

The founders and official representatives of Humanity.

(The) Divine

The All that IS, the Omnipotent Divine, the Omniscient Divines, and Humanity's Omniscient.

Divine Intervention

(As defined by Humanity's experience.)

The act of influencing, assisting, or interfering by a non-member of Humanity.

Fear Itself

It is an entity, though it is not an actual being.
It has consciousness, an awareness of its existence.
It has intelligence, the ability to achieve its own mission.
It is a consciousness, the ruling consciousness on Earth.
It currently serves as Humanity's collective consciousness.

First Intentional Existence

A purposeful existence, consciously chosen and initiated through our rising desire.

Free Will

The allowance and ability to self-govern.

Initial Existence

Our first existence as the Light, initiated and facilitated by our desire to exist.

Mortal Majority

The souls of Humanity.

Multi-Realm Universe

The Universe created by the Omniscient Divines containing the realms of Truth, Unconditional Love, Angelic, Celestial, Universal, Tertiary, and Planetary.

One Divine Mind

The consciousness of the All that IS, aka the Omnipotent Divine.
The highest state of consciousness in all of existence.

Order of Creation

The Universal Path all conscious beings and souls take to expedite an existence.

Peace on Earth

A reality Humanity desires to restore through their collective Awakening.
A reality once lived on Planet Earth before Humanity descended in consciousness.
A reality where warring, violence, discrimination, disease, suffering, and death do not exist.

There

A location created for Humanity's Omniscient to live after the implementation of Humanity's Second Intention. Additionally, it is the current home of Humanity's souls.

Truth

It is what reveals the origin of whom we are and how all existing came into existence.

Unveiled

A state of consciousness that is unaffected by the veil's placement.

(The) **Veil**

A fixed barrier Humanity placed between themselves and all higher consciousness.s

Veiled

A state of consciousness that is limited and burdened by the veil's placement.

About the Author

Ms. Isaac is a teacher, speaker, thinking-outside-of-the-box, problem-solving solution seeker. Her vision is for Humanity to live United as One. Her mission is to inspire Humanity's achievement of peace, through the opening of hearts, minds, and dialogues. In a world where we fear for the future of Planet Earth and our children, she delivers hope to us all by eloquently disclosing the magnificence of our origin.

Ms. Isaac's most endearing quality is her faith in Humanity. She is a steadfast enthusiast and passionate advocate because more than anyone, she believes in our ability to facilitate peace. She proves her allegiance through her daily commitment to prioritize the needs and wellbeing of Humanity above all else, including herself.

My Calling, My Quest (Truth) is the first installment of a series of books Ms. Isaac has written to illustrate and remind us about the brilliance we possess to peacefully exist. For additional information you can visit her at www.MyCallingMyQuest.com.

Made in the USA
Las Vegas, NV
21 February 2021